‘Regional Universities’ and Pedagogy

Gigliola Paviotti

'Regional Universities' and Pedagogy

Graduate Employability in Rural Labour Markets

palgrave
macmillan

Gigliola Paviotti
University of Macerata
Macerata, Italy

ISBN 978-3-030-53679-4 ISBN 978-3-030-53680-0 (eBook)
https://doi.org/10.1007/978-3-030-53680-0

This Palgrave Macmillan imprint is published by the registered company Springer Nature Switzerland AG.
The registered company address is: Gewerbestrasse 11, 6330 Cham, Switzerland

Acknowledgements

My desire to explore more deeply the topic of employability in rural economies originated during my PhD studies in Education at the University of Macerata in central Italy, one of the oldest universities in Europe (founded in 1290), which "serves" a rural and peri-urban region characterised by many of the features defining "rural economy" or "local labour markets".

I am very grateful to graduates of my university, those who have left the region as well as those who have remained, many of whom have uncertain work conditions, and many of whom have chosen different pathways than those for which they studied. They have taught me how transition happens beyond narratives.

My deepest thanks to Professor Alessio Cavicchi, agricultural economist and unique colleague and friend.

I thank Sheila Beatty for editing the English version of the manuscript.

Last but not least, my sincere gratitude to the editors Rebecca Wyde and Eleanor Christie for their professional support and valuable insights throughout the entire process of writing and publication.

Contents

Abbreviations

CEDEFOP	European Centre for the Development of Vocational Training
CF	Cohesion Fund
EC	European Commission
ERDF	European Regional Development Fund
ESF	European Social Fund
EU	European Union
EURES	European Employment Services
EUROSTAT	Statistical Office of the European Communities
HE	Higher Education
ILO	International Labour Organisation
ISCO	International Standard Classification of Occupations
OECD	Organisation for Economic Co-operation and Development
PES	Public Employment Services
RIS3	Research and Innovation Strategies for Smart Specialisation
SDGs	Sustainable Development Goals
SDSN	Sustainable Development Solutions Network
SME	Small and Medium Enterprise
UBC	University-Business Cooperation
WBL	Work-Based Learning
WEF	World Economic Forum
WIL	Work Integrated Learning

List of Tables

Introduction

Much has been written about graduate employability, and the term is common today in government policies, the media, and educational research. Narratives of neoliberal policies advance the idea that graduates should be responsible for readying themselves for work, supported by the education system. As the "societal role" of the university has come to the fore, these institutions have been vested with new functions, and their intrinsic and instrumental values have been discussed widely. Dramatic changes in the world of work have meant that businesses now insist on greater flexibility in hiring, firing, and benefits, demanding workers who can adapt quickly to new job descriptions and responsibilities; this dynamism has left a sizeable sector of the working population at the mercy of uncertain financial and business flows. At the same time, in the interests of economic growth, governments have re-formulated welfare provisions to "rationalise costs", shifting upon citizens the responsibility for almost every aspect of their life, including education and personal development.

During these developments, there has also been a new awareness of the urgent need for sustainability that has motivated countries to commit to achieving the United Nations 17 Sustainable Development Goals for society, the economy, and the environment.

These different needs necessarily intertwine: working towards decent work and economic growth (SDG 8) may demand changes in the economic paradigm; making human settlements inclusive, resilient, and sustainable (SGD 11) entails reviewing the concepts of urban and rural, including employment, health, and mobility.

While we work towards a more socially, economically, and environmentally sustainable planet, we sometimes fail to address some sectors in need of attention, among them, graduate employability in peripheral areas. About half of the territory of the European Union is rural, home to about 20% of the European population. These often-fragile territories are characterised by low innovation and less development, with poor employment prospects. Rural regions of Europe often see an exodus of young people to cities, only partially compensated as older residents return to the countryside. Many EU and national government policies aim to support regional growth through research and innovation ecosystems based on local and specialised resources and capacities. Universities are expected to be crucial players in regional innovation, contributing through research, education, and formation of human capital, but how this role should be played out in urban and rural regions remains unclear. More specifically, how can a university located in rural or peri-urban setting support graduate employability to the same extent and with the same outcomes as a university based in a major city? Overall, it is unclear how human settlement can be "inclusive, resilient and sustainable" in rural areas where their most educated young members find it impossible to contribute to the local economy and feel forced to seek better prospects in urban centres.

This study seeks to contribute to understanding how narratives of employability should be re-framed to support sustainability. It focuses on a topic in part neglected by research: how can graduate employability be fostered in European rural economies? Are there teaching and learning practices that support the employability of graduates in rural labour markets?

The title of this book sets "Regional Universities" in quotation marks because this work includes, but does not focus on, the model of regional universities as formulated in the literature. Instead, it addresses higher-education institutions that deal with rural or peri-urban territories in their regional action. Since different countries vary on their definitions of "urban" or "regional" or "rural" universities, the book title uses the word "regional" to point out the limits and opportunities of the reference territories of universities.

This work is largely explorative and seeks not so much to propose easy solutions as to open a dialogue among different disciplines on the very complex topic of the employability of graduates in rural areas.

The book is organised as follows. Chapter 1 provides general background and describes employability in the context of social and economic changes of recent years. Chapter 2 outlines the macro-level of policies in education, regional development, and sustainability issues, and Chap. 3 describes the concept of "rural" and delineates the characteristics of rural economies and employment. Chapters 4 and 5 focus on the meso-level of graduate employability, namely higher education and business, while Chap. 6 describes the micro-level of individual students and graduates. Chapter 7 explores pedagogies that support the increase of employability potential for rural economies. Finally, the Conclusions highlight the need for further dialogue among components of society to reach system-level thinking to tackle global issues, both at the vertical level of policies and at the horizontal level of stakeholders.

CHAPTER 1

Graduate Employability

Abstract The concept of employability ranges from the individual to the global dimensions, and encompasses several domains. This chapter outlines the key socio-economic transformations that have modified transition pathways between education and work, and describes the changing nature of jobs and careers. Following major changes in the nature of employment, the concept of employability has been accordingly re-formulated: in this context, the nature of jobs for university graduates has changed towards new professional roles and positions that are not yet fixed. The chapter introduces the main shift from employment to employability as a consequence of new policies implemented, in particular in Western countries, then analyses the concept of employability that has resulted from socio-economic changes, including the entrepreneurial components, and concludes with the analysis of "university graduate jobs" as conceived today.

Keywords Employability • Labour market • Entrepreneurship • Graduate jobs

1.1 From Employment to Employability

Transitions from education to work[1] were relatively stable for most of the past century, as a consequence of established education and training programs, welfare, labour market systems, and family structures across

G. Paviotti, *'Regional Universities' and Pedagogy*,
https://doi.org/10.1007/978-3-030-53680-0_1

Europe. Even if the patterns of transitions were different across countries (e.g. a *parallel* model in Germany or a *sequential* model in France), similar patterns of transition from education to work were identified in cohorts of young people as "cumulative" experiences (Muller and Gangl 2003).

The change in cultural, social, and economic systems due to globalisation, technological change, and neoliberal policies in Western countries has deeply affected the social life and its values, in a process that has been defined as "detraditionalisation" (Heelas et al. 1996), "individualisation" (Beck and Ritter 1992), and "disembedding" (Giddens 1991). The focus on the "self" has been translated into individual experiences of transitions, depending on either "choice biographies" (Du Bois Reymond 1995) or new patterns of vulnerability and perceptions of uncertainty (Furlong et al. 2003; Wyn and White 1997; Furlong et al. 2006). As Cieslik and Pollock (2002, p. 3) argue: "In place of these collective guides and traditional institutions are much more individualised identities and biographies where individuals have a greater scope beyond traditional markers of class, race, and gender to create complex subjective lifestyles".

If no new "single model of transition" can be identified, some elements, common among countries, can be identified as follows (Raffe 2011):

- The transition process takes much longer (typically from around age 15 to age 25, OECD 2000).
- In all countries the position of young entrants to the labour market differs from that of adults, and in many respects is less favourable.
- Education plays particular roles in preparing young people for the labour market.
- In all countries, transitions are differentiated and unequal, and different categories of young people have different experiences.

To understand the change in transitions from university to the world of work, the dramatic change of the labour market should be considered first. Since the 1970s, the automatisation of work and other factors have led to a downsizing of the labour market, particularly in manufacturing and construction. Manufacturing in particular was a strong field for Western labour markets, and job loss cumulated during the years of recession (2008–2009). Structural changes affected the market, which has shifted from an industrial society to a knowledge-based economy, driven by technological innovation. This shift involved a radical change in the conception of human resources: mass production and consumption, which required a large number of employees, are no longer central to economic growth, and "knowledge-intensive" companies, based on technological innovation and a highly skilled workforce, have taken the fore (Stewart 2001). According to Drucker (1993), in the "post-capitalist" society "the basic economic resource [...] is and will be knowledge" (1993, p. 7), intended as knowledge "for doing", or knowledge "in action", after centuries of "knowledge for being".[2] The rise of the 'knowledge worker' has dominated the discourse on human capital in recent years. Although a shared definition of this term has not yet been agreed upon, it can generally be said that knowledge workers have as main capital their knowledge, and possess hard and soft skills that allow them to apply knowledge to a task or job. They are able to find, process, handle, and use information within a lifelong process of learning. The impact of the knowledge economy on the labour market, as in other spheres of the individual, has of course been disruptive. As the worker owns the capital, hierarchies and powers are modified (managers vs leaders), centralised organisations become decentralised organisations, sectors become permeable, and companies are not always able to define to which sector they belong (Phillips et al. 2017). The knowledge-based economy offers a great promise that anyone "skilled enough" or smart enough or committed enough can achieve the higher positions in professional settings, with incomes more and more polarised between the "winners" (those who achieve the higher positions) and the "losers" (those who do not) (Brown and Hesketh 2004). The process and its implications became more visible during the years of economic crisis, but the effects on the labour market had already started in the final decades of the twentieth century, when finding or keeping a job was a challenge for many individuals (Rothwell and Rothwell 2017). Also, the nature of jobs has changed from permanent to temporary positions. The ILO report 2019 (World Employment and Social Outlook Trends 2019) highlights how in Northern, Southern, and Western Europe, although with differences from country to country, there is a general shift towards temporary or part-time contracts, with uncertain welfare conditions and social protection and with a certain degree of risk of poverty (2017, p. 51). In 2016, a study for the European Parliament stated that "all employment relationships are at some risk of precariousness" (European Parliament 2016, p. 11), however assigning a higher level of risk to temporary agency and posted work and informal/undeclared work (e.g. zero hours contracts), and a low risk to permanent positions. According to European data, permanent contracts accounted in 2018 for the 85.8% of the working population aged 15–64+, temporary workers accounted for 14.2% of the working population (women share 50%), with remarkable differences between countries (from 26.8% of Spain to 1.6% of Lithuania). Part-time work increased from 14.9% in 2002 to 18.5% in 2018 (Eurostat 2018).

In average, those possessing higher educational attainments have more chances to work in a permanent position (64% versus 48% of low-skilled workers) (European Parliament 2016, elaboration on Eurostat 2014 data-sets). However, youths are generally disadvantaged in access to permanent positions, in particular in times of economic crisis (O'Higgins 2012; Michoń 2019; Verd et al. 2019), and are more likely to get low-paid jobs. This also applies to those having completed higher education (OECD 2019).

The share of permanent contracts varies by economic activity: the higher share is observable in manufacturing, public administration, and education, the lower share in the service sector, in which part-time working and seasonal contracts are very common (OECD 2019). Self-employment, including freelancers, is rather common in agriculture, fishery, and forestry (53%), followed by ICT, real estate and financial and professional services (23%), and retail and trade (18%) (European Parliament 2016). It should be noted in respect to these data that "the share of manufacturing value added in overall GDP declined from 20% in 1995 to 16% in 2011 (following a long term trend), whereas the share of business services increased from about 14% to 18% over the same period for the whole economy" (ECSIP Consortium 2014, p. 9; OECD 2017).

New forms of work, mostly related to digital transformation and to globalisation, also recently emerged, impacting on corporate organisation and production methods (Degryse 2016): a well-known example of a range of "new occupations" is represented by the platform work (Eurofound 2018).[3] Platform work is defined as "a form of employment that uses an online platform to enable organisations or individuals to access other organisations or individuals to solve specific problems or to provide specific services in exchange for payment" (Eurofound 2018, p. 15). The platform work is associated with the growth of self-employed (or freelancers), who trade individual tasks and commissions online. The phenomenon, which seems to be not yet widely spread in Europe[4] but growing at a constant speed, concerns defined targets of the population: Pesole et al. (2018), by comparing results from previous studies (Ipeirotis 2010; Eurofound 2015; Huws et al. 2017), conclude that platform workers are "significantly more educated than the comparable general population" (p. 26). In the group of those having the platform work as the main source of income, the 55.1% holds an education credential ISCED 5 or above. This data could be explained considering that the Internet is used more by higher-educated people or by taking into account that they belong mostly to the younger part of the population (workers below 34 years compose the half of the platform workers population, Pesole et al. 2018) that young people have more difficulties to find a regular employment and rely on this type of activity to make a living or to increase incomes (Huws et al. 2017). Some authors also highlight advantages of the gig economy,[5] which includes platform work, like the opportunity to have flexible work-schedules, autonomy, and feeling of having control over one's own professional life (McKinsey 2017; Broughton et al. 2018; Dazzi 2019).

Following major social and economic changes, the labour market has thus shifted from employment to employability, where contracts of loyalty for job security and career progressions (Cappelli 1999; Brown and Hesketh 2004)[6] have been replaced by flexible and insecure work conditions, and employability as a term shifted from the objective of securing one stable and reliable position or career (Feintuch 1955) to the capability to find and to remain employed through a series of jobs and careers. This also reflects the view of the companies, which are not able or willing to offer long-term career opportunities (Brown and Hesketh 2004, p. 27): in other words, while in the past century the dominant culture was steady employment, often with the same corporation for the worker's lifetime (Magnum 1976), today's careers have become increasingly less predictable, more "boundaryless," and "protean".

One of the definitions of a boundaryless career is

> a career that is not confined to a single occupation or organisation but involves movement across traditional boundaries. This will involve changing jobs and employment status and may also include periods outside the conventional labour market, either concentrating on family roles or undertaking a career break. (Heery and Noon 2017)

Other authors look more at the different organisational settings of the companies, which have moved from hierarchical progressions to careers in which occupational, departmental, and organisational boundaries are crossed (DeFillippi and Arthur 1996; Gunz et al. 2000), where competency-based perspectives are crucial to employment and career (DeFillippi and Arthur 1996).

In 1996, Arthur and Rousseau defined six specific meanings for the boundaryless career (Roper et al. 2010, pp. 662–663):

- Movement across the boundaries of separate employers;
- Drawing validation from outside the present employer;
- Sustained by networks or information that are external to the current employer;
- Breaking traditional organisational career boundaries;
- Rejection of traditional career opportunities for personal or family reasons;
- Perceiving a boundaryless future regardless of structural constraints.

Later, Sullivan and Arthur (2006) generalised it to comprise physical (objective) and psychological (subjective) mobility, which are two interdependent continua in career worlds.

Likewise, a "protean career" is driven by the individual, not by organisations. The concept dates back to 1976, and was further developed by the same Hall, who defined "the protean career as one driven by the needs of the individual rather than the organisation and characterised by frequent change, autonomy, and self-direction" (Hall 2001, p. 4). The protean career is therefore based on two main attitudes: it is values-driven, prizing individual values over organisational values, and it is self-directed, marked by independence in managing vocational behaviour (Briscoe et al. 2006).

The boundaryless and protean concepts have dominated the discourse on careers in recent decades, following economic and political trends towards a pathway of globalised trade and deregulation of markets, including the labour market (Roper et al. 2010; Kuttner 2018). Greater responsibility lies in the hands of the individuals, who must enact own career journeys showing proactivity, self-awareness, and life design abilities (Inkson and Arthur 2001; Inkson and Elkin 2008).

The narrative of the "new careers", or careers in the new economy, tends to highlight the positive side for the individual—autonomy, freedom of choice, and self-fulfilment. However, the emphasis on "self-direction" in careers places the onus of "being employable" on the individual (Keep and Mayhew 2010), who is asked to undertake a never-ending process of life design and re-design. In today's society, unemployment is considered a personal weakness more than a collective responsibility, ignoring in this way the dynamics and the dynamism of the labour markets (Serrano Pascual 2001). Further, the idea that individuals with the same credentials and skills compete equally for jobs is at best naïve: several studies have investigated the challenges faced by individuals from a disadvantaged background as they compete in the labour market (Bourdieu and Passeron 1977; Furlong and Cartmel 2005; Holmes 2011; Tomlinson 2008). Social position, which entails codes and languages, but also different personal networks, gender, and location, play a role in the process of recruiting, which claims to use "scientific" (objective and rigorous) tools, but still has strong relational and contextualised features, as pointed out by Brown and Hesketh (2004), who defined the selection process as "the science of gut feeling".

1.2 Defining Employability

Although employability and its components are popular in academic and policy discourses, no univocal definition has been agreed upon.

Gazier (2001) identified seven phases in the evolution of the meaning of employability from 1900 to today, from a policy perspective: the latest versions, having their onset in the 1900s, are defined as ***initiative employability*** and ***interactive employability***. The first is linked with the capacity of the individual to gather and activate resources around his/her project, and it is very close to the entrepreneurial model, while the second is focused on "the relative capacity of an individual to achieve meaningful employment given the interaction between personal characteristics and the labour market" and is linked to the implementation of so-called active measures of labour.

Looking at general definitions applicable to individuals, several can be found in the literature, as for example:

> For the individual, employability depends on the knowledge, skills and aptitudes they possess, the way they use those assets and present them to employers and the context (e.g. personal circumstances and labour market environment) within which they seek work. (Hillage and Pollard 1998, p. 2)

> [the employability of individuals will be defined] as the relative chances of getting and maintaining different kinds of employment. (Brown and Hesketh 2004, p. 25)

or, applied to graduates:

> a set of achievements—skills, understandings and personal attributes—that make graduates more likely to gain employment and be successful in their chosen occupations, which benefits themselves, the workforce, the community and the economy. (Yorke 2004)

Sin and Neave (2016) argue that the term is a "floating signifier" in Lévi-Strauss' sense of the term (1950), i.e. "a construct that accommodates different and often contending meanings"; according to Cremin (2010, p. 133) employability is an "empty signifier", that "draws together the fluff or a number of unconnected words, into a relationship with one another".

The concept and term relate to the labour market overall, not specifically to transitions from education to work: a considerable body of literature discusses employability of employees in order to ensure that workers are able to face the fluctuating requirements of the market (Van Dam 2004; Fugate et al. 2004; Van der Heijde and Van der Heijden 2006). Employability is, in fact, a lifelong process.

Thijssen et al. (2008) distinguished between three perspectives from which employability can be viewed, namely (1) *societal or national*, referring to employment rates of a country; (2) *organisational*, the company level, where the focus is on matching supply and demand in a changing organisation; and (3) *individual*, where a person seeks to "acquire and to keep an attractive job in the internal or external labour market" (p. 168).

Likewise, Tomlinson and Holmes (2017), focusing on the transition from student to graduate, also define three levels, namely (1) *macro-level*, which is the structural system level related to neoliberal policies and to how educational systems are coordinated within the framework; (2) *meso-level*, which refers to how employability and people's work-related activities are mediated by institutional-level processes located within both educational and organisational domains; and (3) *micro-level*, which is constructed at the personal level and encompasses a range of subjective, biographical and psycho-social dynamics, as well as the individual's cultural profile and background.

1.2.1 *Macro-Level*

The macro-level analysis, as briefly explained in the previous paragraph, shows governments that "seek to enable rather than provide" (Edwards 2003), or that seek to promote personal mobility through active policies (Gazier 2001; Garsten and Jacobsson 2003). While the responsibility of being employable is primarily on individuals, education systems are asked to support the building of employable citizens.

1.2.2 *Meso-Level*

At the meso-level, the necessary relation between education and business systems is the centre of attention: in fact, as straightforwardly pointed out by Brown and Hesketh "the acid test of employability is employment" (2004, p. 18). Employability cannot be defined per se in terms of individual values, skills, and capabilities, because even an excellent candidate can remain unemployed in a very negative labour market. The relative dimension needs to be considered: external and economic factors which may be sector- or region-specific (Saxenian 1994; Harvey 2000) can affect the actual employment of the individual, regardless of that person's employability potential (Harvey 2001; Holmes 2011). In the knowledge-based economy, learning is only a pre-requisite for obtaining and retaining a job (Garsten and Jacobsson 2003; Sin and Neave 2016); higher education, which was both necessary and sufficient to achieve a stable position in the labour market, particularly when the public sector was stronger, is now necessary, but often insufficient (Sin and Neave 2016, p. 2; Brown and Hesketh 2004, p. 30). The "massification" of higher education (Scott 1995) weakened the power of credentials (Brown and Hesketh 2004) and required the workforce to be equipped with different forms of skills, often related to personal qualities (Hassard et al. 2008; Purcell et al. 2002). The influence of the requests from the labour market for fit-for-purpose graduates is still a controversial issue leading to tensions between employers and academics (Barnett 2000; Rae 2004), and also in the views and expectations of students (Finch et al. 2016). This tension is unavoidable, because, as Tomlinson and Holmes pointed out, work organisations "mediate the ways in which graduates' career progression and employability are played out in context" (2017, p. 10).

A significant body of literature is devoted to discussions about skills, ranging from those considered the most significant for employers (Purcell et al. 2002; Slade 2014; El Mansour and Dean 2016; Wesley et al. 2017), to the difficulty of teaching and assessing them (Knight and Yorke 2003; Huber et al. 2007), and the "vagueness" of their definition (Mason et al. 2009). This ongoing debate has led to a great fragmentation of concepts and interpretations. The same terms are unclear: for example, "generic skills" is used interchangeably with "core skills", "basic skills", "transferable skills", and "employability skills" (Cabellero et al. 2011).

Similarly, there is a lack of common understanding about the meaning of "employability skills", which of course include hard "technical" skills, also encompass the hazily defined aspects of soft skills, interpersonal skills, and career skills.

Several studies and government initiatives have provided frameworks for employability skills, such as the soft skills clusters by Crawford et al. (2012), the U.S. Department of Education (2013), and the Australian "Employability Skills for the Future". Within higher education as well, various and diverse forms of skills sets have been proposed to support graduate employability (e.g. Hager and Holland 2006; Yorke and Knight 2006; Harvey 2000; see Suleman 2016 for a complete analysis). The debate, however, has been more focused on the concept of "graduate attributes". Bowden et al.'s (2000) commonly cited definition states that graduate attributes are "the qualities, skills and understandings a university community agrees its students would desirably develop during their time at the institution and, consequently, shape the contribution they are able to make to their profession and as a citizen". The concept includes the formative value of universities, whose aim is to educate citizens, not merely to train workers (Morley 2001; Leonard 2000). Further definitions related to graduates include the concepts of "graduate identity" (Holmes 2001) and "graduateness" (Steur et al. 2016).

The concept of graduate identity starts from the acknowledgement that assessment of skills and attributes cannot succeed, as no performance indicator can capture a "skill" or "attribute" (Holmes 2001, 2011). Holmes draws upon the notions of a) type of activity, and b) kind of person doing the activity (in context), noting that in the process there is always someone observing and interpreting the situation and the people in the situation—then their identity. The process has a relational nature: when graduates apply for a job, they should be *identified* as a graduate, which does not mean "merely possessing a degree certificate" (Holmes 2011, p. 7). The relational process of identification is based on the interaction between individuals who claim/disclaim a particular identity, and the affirmation/disaffirmation of such a claim.

Graduateness refers to "something generic that is developed through the university experience and is expected to be achieved by graduates" (Steur et al. 2016, p. 2). While acknowledging that university equips students with skills, Steur et al. consider that the student develops high cognitive abilities, which include the value given to knowledge, that enables "depth of skills that otherwise would remain superficial" (2016, p. 5).

1.2.3 *Micro-Level*

Looking at the micro-level of employability, the focus is on individuals. In past years the dominant discourse has been around skills, on the assumption that graduates possessing the most required skills are more employable. The correlation is obviously not so direct: an individual is more than a sum of skills acquired in formal education. Much research has stressed that graduate employability is a broad and complex concept (Holmes 2011; Brown and Hesketh 2004; Jackson 2016).

A more comprehensive approach uses the dimension of "capitals" (Tomlinson 2013, 2017; Clark et al. 2011; Williams et al. 2016) to understand what shapes the graduates' transitional activities and access to the labour market.

Brown and Hesketh (2004) argue that "personal capital" in relation to employability depends "on a combination of hard currencies, including credentials, work experience, sporting or music achievements, etc. and soft currencies, including interpersonal skills, charisma, appearance and accent" (p. 35). These currencies are mediated by the self (family, gender, ethnicity, values) and the narratives of employability, in particular from the employers' side.

According to Tomlinson (2013, 2017), we can identify at least three broad "employability capitals", key resources that favour transitions from education to work:

- Human capital: this relates directly to hard skills and technological knowledge acquired by graduates during the study years;
- Social capital: this is related to social relations and contacts (networks or social ties that support graduates in getting closer to targeted employment);

- Cultural capital: cultural knowledge, behaviours, and awareness of the enterprises' environment and the work culture of the place.

Two further capitals of relevance to the labour market complement the three key capitals:

- Identity capital: this refers to the investment of the graduates to their future career, and connect their personal identity to targeted employment;
- Psychological capital: this refers particularly to the levels of adaptability and resilience against a challenging labour market.

Tomlinson defines capitals as "key resources, accumulated through graduates' educational, social and initial employment experiences, and which equip them favourably when transitioning to the labour market" (2017, p. 18).

While the formation of capitals is linked with the life of the individual, a greater contribution is provided by higher education. Higher-education institutions also are multi-level and multi-faceted organisations, which offer not only courses and teaching, but also cultural, political, and social experiences. Universities are partly a "landscape of practice" (Jackson 2016, referring to Wenger's concept) where students have opportunities for personal development. Work-based learning, internships, student associations, and so on contribute to the development of networks, acquisition of business knowledge, and formation of professional identity (or, according to Jackson, to pre-professional identity building).

1.3 Employability as Entrepreneurial Process

Another phenomenon that has been explored in the literature in the past decades is entrepreneurship. Once only a theme examined in business schools, it has become a policy topic in education, in efforts to prepare citizens to be "entrepreneurial". Also, in this case, the self is emphasised: individuals are expected to be responsible for their own career trajectory, as an entrepreneur is.

The European Union has also made a strong effort in entrepreneurship education (European Commission 2013, 2014, 2016) but views entrepreneurship not as "being an entrepreneur" but as "being an enterprising individual". Relations between entrepreneurship and employability have been widely debated (e.g. Gibb 2002; Sewell and Dacre Pool 2010; Rae 2007), and there is consensus on the idea that an entrepreneurial mindset is an asset in any kind of employment (Moreland 2006). According to Moreland (2006, p. 5), if employability is defined as "a set of achievements, understandings and personal attributes that make individuals more likely to gain employment and be successful in their chosen occupations (Yorke 2004, p. 7)", then entrepreneurship is "a subset of employability". Self-employment should be considered as well: self-employment is increasingly an employment choice and shares a number of factors with entrepreneurship, although not in terms of the creation of a new company (Kolvereid 1996, 2016). Finally, the concept of "intrapreneurship" (Antoncic and Hisrich 2003) describes entrepreneurial behaviour within existing companies.

The European Union has also provided a number of resources to support education and training systems, starting with the EntreComp, a framework of reference for entrepreneurship, addressing 5 competences along an 8-level progression model and with a comprehensive list of 442 learning outcomes (Bacigalupo et al. 2016). Other resources include the Guide for Educators (European Commission 2014), the HEInnovate Scheme (EC-OECD), and the EvalueComp, to assess the impact of entrepreneurship programmes in higher education (under development, 2019). HEInnovate supports entrepreneurial training (European Commission 2009), and funding schemes, in particular under the Erasmus+ programme.

While Europe has a fairly clear definition of entrepreneurship education, internationally its purpose and components are less shared, and often the terms "entrepreneurial", "entrepreneurship", and "enterprise education" are used interchangeably (Draycott and Rae 2011; Mwasalwiba 2010; Morselli 2019). In North America, entrepreneurship education is more focused on preparing individuals to create a business, as entrepreneurship is viewed as the key to economic growth. Typical of the clear definition that prevails is that of Neck and Corbett (2018, p. 10): "we define entrepreneurship education as developing the mindset, skillset, and practice necessary for starting new ventures".

Thus, there are two streams of research about entrepreneurship in relation to learning (Blenker et al. 2008): the first focuses on pedagogy, while the second focuses on universities as educational providers and their role within the business and social context.

The stream of research on pedagogy explores "internal" questions of didactics and pedagogy. According to Wang and Chugh (2014), who carried out a systematic analysis of literature on teaching and learning methods, the most applied theories are experiential learning (Kolb 1984), transformative learning (Mezirow 1997), and situated learning (Lave and Wenger 1991). Other authors have indicated expansive learning (Engeström 2015) as the most suitable learning theory for forming entrepreneurial graduates. Thus, in general, the most suitable pedagogical approaches to support the acquisition of entrepreneurial behaviour are those included under the umbrella of "active pedagogies". A structured theory of learning for entrepreneurship, however, has not been agreed upon, and some arguments still exist about the possibility of "teaching entrepreneurship" (Henry et al. 2005; Klein and Bullock 2006) and how to train teachers to do it (Fiet 2000).

The stream of research on the role of the university is perhaps best represented by studies on the concept of the entrepreneurial university, in the overall frame of triple/quadruple helix metaphors (Etzkowitz 2008; Carayannis and Campbell 2009; Ranga and Etzkowitz 2013).

In both streams of research, the focus is still on the student and the graduate: learning entrepreneurship (the acquisition of entrepreneurial skills or behaviour) means becoming competent and ready for the market, or, in other words, being employable.

1.4 What Are Graduate Jobs?

As we look at graduate employability, we should ask ourselves what can be considered jobs for graduate in our age. Following economic and social changes, the professions defined as jobs for graduates have also changed over time. Purcell and Elias (2004, p. 7) proposed four categories of graduate employment:

- Traditional graduate occupations, which refer to professions like medical practitioners, higher-education and secondary education teachers, and other scientific and technical occupations;
- Modern graduate occupations, which include professionals in IT and vocational areas, primary school teachers, management, and new administrative posts in the public and private sectors;
- Occupations for new graduates, which include sales and marketing managers, health practitioners (e.g. physiotherapists), management accountants, and welfare work;

- Niche graduate occupations, defined as jobs "in areas of employment in which most workers do not have degrees, but within which there are stable or growing specialist niches for which graduates are sought", which include leisure and sports managers, hotel and accommodation managers, and senior administrators in education establishments.

Further, Purcell et al. (2013), while acknowledging that "it is not possible to provide a universal definition of what constitutes a graduate job as a general taxonomic category" (2013, p. 10), proposed three categories of job classification based on the skills and experience required to perform the task, and the link with higher education:

- Experts: occupations in knowledge-intensive sectors, such as chemical scientists, engineers, pharmacists and so on.
- Orchestrators: defined as "jobs that require them to draw on and orchestrate their knowledge and the knowledge of others to evaluate information, assess options, plan, make decisions and coordinate the contributions of others to achieve objectives", such as managers
- Communicators: defined as jobs that require "interactive skills that may be based on interpersonal skills, creative skills or high-level technological knowledge, capacity to access and manipulate information and/or an understanding of how to communicate information effectively to achieve objectives", for example, marketing professionals or web design professionals.

This proposal, developed as part of the FutureTrack survey,[7] is one of the few offered to define "graduate jobs". Professional positions that until 20 years ago were accessible to candidates with higher secondary education diplomas today require at least a bachelor's degree, because of the combination of degree inflation, oversaturation of the labour market, and the digital revolution, which have given rise to professional profiles that did not exist a few years ago (Brown and Hesketh 2004; Tomlinson 2008). While narratives of employability stress the need for a skilled workforce for the knowledge economy, or new economy, actual employment results often indicate a phenomenon of overeducation and/or underemployment throughout Western countries, especially Southern countries. Overeducation is defined as "the extent to which individuals possesses a level of education in excess of that which is required for their particular job" (McGuinness 2006; Flisi et al. 2014).[8] Some nations (e.g. Spain; see Ortiz 2010; Dolado et al. 2002) experience difficulty in maintaining or increasing investment in human capital to stimulate labour productivity. Overeducated individuals can experience frustration, low levels of job satisfaction, and reduced wellbeing (Artés et al. 2014).

Notes

1. The International Labour Office defines transition as "the passage of a young person (aged 15 to 29 years) from the end of schooling to the first fixed-term or satisfactory employment", where "fixed term is defined in terms of duration of contract or expected length of tenure" (opposite to temporary job), and satisfactory, as subjective element, refers to "a job that the respondent considers to "fit" to his desired employment path at that moment in time" (ILO 2010, pp. 3–4).
2. Drucker identifies three phases of shift in the conception of knowledge—the Industrial Revolution, the Productivity Revolution, and the Management Revolution—concluding that in all those phases knowledge was generalist, while in the knowledge-based society (KBE), knowledge is highly specialised. In fact, if the techné or craft was traditionally not included in the concept of knowledge, as learnt by experience, in the KBE craft is "specialised knowledge", which is called "discipline". Disciplines structure methodologies; methodologies "convert anecdote into information"; information can be converted into skill that can be taught and learnt (Drucker 1993, pp. 41, 42).
3. Eurofound (2018) identifies nine new forms of work, namely strategic employee sharing, job sharing, interim management, casual work, ICT-based mobile work, voucher-based work, portfolio work, platform work, and collaborative self-employment.
4. Pesole et al. (2018) define platform workers as "those who earn 50% or more of their income via platforms and/or work via platforms more than 20 hours a week" and estimate that they represent the 2% of the adult population (p. 18).
5. The term "gig economy" refers to the freelance economy since the 2009, refer-ring to the several micro-jobs that people in financial distress carried out during the years of the crisis; it originates from the "gig work" of jazz musicians in the 1920s (Financial Times, Year in a word: 2015, "Gig economy").

6. Of note is the concept of the "psychological contract," which organisational studies define as the "The unspoken promise, not present in the small print of the employment contract, of what the employer gives, what employees give in return, and vice versa" (Baruch 2001, p. 544): this type of tacit agreement has been swept away.
7. Futuretrack is the most extensive investigation survey of the relationship between higher education and employment in the UK: https://warwick.ac.uk/fac/soc/ier/futuretrack/what-is/.
8. . In Italy (2018), overeducation concerned 42.1% of the employed graduates; it is not strictly linked to access to work but continues over time, affecting 40% of graduates at +6 years from the degree (ISTAT 2019). In Europe, overeducation ranged from 38% in 2001 to 53% in 2009 (Eurofound 2014).

References

Antoncic, B., & Hisrich, R. D. (2003). Clarifying the Intrapreneurship Concept. *Journal of Small Business and Enterprise Development, 10*(1), 7–24.

Artés, J., Salinas-Jiménez, M. M., & Salinas-Jiménez, J. (2014). Small Fish in a Big Pond or Big Fish in a Small Pond? The Effects of Educational Mismatch on Subjective Wellbeing. *Social Indicators Research, 119*(2), 771–789.

Bacigalupo, M., Kampylis, P., Punie, Y., & Van den Brande, G. (2016). *EntreComp: The Entrepreneurship Competence Framework*. Luxembourg: Publication Office of the European Union.

Barnett, R. (2000). Thinking the University, Again. *Educational Philosophy and Theory, 32*(3), 319–326.

Baruch, Y. (2001). Employability: A Substitute for Loyalty? *Human Resource Development International, 4*(4), 543–566.

Beck, U., & Ritter, M. (1992). *Risk Society: Towards a New Modernity*. London: Sage Publications.

Blenker, P., Dreisler, P., Færgemann, H. M., & Kjeldsen, J. (2008). A Framework for Developing Entrepreneurship Education in a University Context. *International Journal of Entrepreneurship and Small Business, 5*(1), 45–63.

Bourdieu, P., & Passeron, J. (1977). *Reproduction in Education, Society and Culture*. London: Sage.

Bowden, J., Hart, G., King, B., Trigwell, K., & Watts, O. (2000). *Generic Capabilities of ATN University Graduates*. Canberra: Australian Government Department of Education, Training and Youth Affairs.

Briscoe, J. P., Hall, D. T., & DeMuth, R. L. F. (2006). Protean and Boundaryless Careers: An Empirical Exploration. *Journal of Vocational Behavior, 69*, 30–47.

Broughton, A., Gloster, R., Marvell, R., Green, M., Langley, J., & Martin, A. (2018). *The Experiences of Individuals in the Gig Economy*. London: Department for Business, Energy & Industrial Strategy.

Brown, P., & Hesketh, A. (2004). *The Mismanagement of Talent: Employability and Jobs in the Knowledge Economy*. Oxford: Oxford University Press.

Cabellero, C. L., Walker, A., & Fuller Tyszkiewicz, M. (2011). The Work Readiness Scale (WRS): Developing a Measure to Assess Work Readiness in College Graduates. *Journal of Teaching and Learning for Graduate Employability, 2*(2), 41–54.

Cappelli, P. (1999). *The New Deal of Work: Managing the Market-Driven Workforce*. Boston, MA: Harvard Business School Books.

Carayannis, E. G., & Campbell, D. F. J. (2009). 'Mode 3' and 'Quadruple Helix': Toward a 21st Century Fractal Innovation Ecosystem. *International Journal of Technology Management, 46*(3/4), 201–223.

Cieslik, M., & Pollock, G. (2002). *Young People in Risk Society: The Restructuring of Youth Identities and Transitions in Late Modernity*. Burlington, VT: Ashgate Publishing Limited.

Clark, M., Zukas, M., & Lent, N. (2011). Becoming an IT Person: Field, Habitus and Capital in the Transition from University to Work. *Vocations and Learning, 4*(2), 133–150.

Crawford, P., Lang, S., Fink, W., Dalton, R., & Fielitz, L. (2012). *Comparative Analysis of Soft Skills. What is Important for New Graduates?* East Lansing, MI: Michigan State University College of Agriculture and Natural Resources.

Cremin, C. (2010). Never Employable Enough: The (Im)possibility of Satisfying the Boss's Desire. *Organization, 17*, 131.

Dazzi, D. (2019). GIG Economy in Europe. *Italian Labour Law e-Journal, 12*(2), 67–122.

DeFillippi, R. J., & Arthur, M. B. (1996). Boundaryless Contexts and Careers: A Competency-Based Perspective. In M. B. Arthur & D. M. Rousseau (Eds.), *The Boundaryless Career: A New Employment Principle for a New Organizational Era* (pp. 116–131). New York, NY: Oxford University Press.

Degryse, C. (2016). *Digitalisation of the Economy and Its Impact on Labour Markets*. Working Paper 2016.02, European Trade Union Institute.

Dolado, J. J., García-Serrano, C., & Jimeno, J. F. (2002). Drawing Lessons from the Boom of Temporary Jobs in Spain. *The Economic Journal, 112*(480), F270–F295.

Draycott, M. C., & Rae, D. (2011). Enterprise Education in Schools and the Role of Competency Frameworks. *International Journal of Entrepreneurial Behavior & Research, 17*(2), 127–145.

Drucker, P. (1993). *Post-Capitalist Society*. Oxford: Butterworth-Heinemann.

Du Bois Reymond, M. (1995). Future Orientations of Dutch Youth: The Emergence of a Choice Biography. In A. Cavalli & O. Galland (Eds.), *Youth in Europe*. London: Pinter.

Edwards, R. (2003). Ordering Subjects: Actor-Networks and Intellectual Technologies in Lifelong Learning. *Studies in the Education of Adults, 35*(1), 54–67.

El Mansour, B., & Dean, J. C. (2016). Employability Skills as Perceived by Employers and University. Faculty in the Fields of Human Resource Development (HRD) for Entry Level Graduate Jobs. *Journal of Human Resource and Sustainability Studies, 4*, 39–49.

Engeström, Y. (2015). *Learning by Expanding*. Cambridge: Cambridge University Press.

ECSIP Consortium. (2014). *Study on the relation between industry and services in terms of productivity and value creation*. Study for the Directorate-General for Enterprise and Industry, Vienna 30th of October 2014. https://ec.europa.eu/docsroom/documents/8528/attachments/1/translations/en/renditions/native

Etzkowitz, H. (2008). *The Triple Helix: University–Industry–Government Innovation In Action*. London: Routledge.

Eurofound. (2014). *Mapping Youth Transitions in Europe*. Luxembourg: Publications Office of the European Union.

Eurofound. (2015). *New forms of employment*. Luxembourg: Publications Office of the European Union.

Eurofound. (2018). *Overview of New Forms of Employment 2018 Update*. Luxembourg: Publications Office of the European Union.

European Commission. (2009). *Entrepreneurship in Vocational Education and Training. Final report of the Expert Group*. Brussels.

European Commission. (2013). *Entrepreneurship 2020 Action Plan. Reigniting the Entrepreneurial Spirit in Europe*. Brussels.

European Commission. (2014). *Entrepreneurship Education: A Guide for Educators*. Brussels.

European Commission. (2016). *A New Skills Agenda for Europe*. Brussels.

European Parliament. (2016). *Precarious Employment in Europe: Patterns, Trends and Policy Strategies*. Directorate General for Internal Policies, European Union.

Feintuch, A. (1955). Improving the Employability and Attitudes of "Difficult-to-Place" Persons. *Psychological Monographs: General and Applied, 69*(7), 1–20.

Fiet, J. O. (2000). The Pedagogical Side of Entrepreneurship Theory. *Journal of Business Venturing, 16*, 101–117.

Finch, D. J., Peacock, M., Levallet, N., & Foster, W. (2016). A Dynamic Capabilities View of Employability: Exploring the Drivers of Competitive Advantage for University Graduates. *Education + Training, 58*(1), 61–81.

Flisi, S., Goglio, V., Meroni, E., Rodrigues, M., & Vera-Toscano, E. (2014). *Occupational Mismatch in Europe: Understanding Overeducation and Overskilling for Policy Making*. Ispra: European Commission, Joint Research Centre, Institute for the Protection and Security of the Citizen.

Fugate, M., Kinicki, A. J., & Ashforth, B. E. (2004). Employability: A Psycho-Social Construct, Its Dimensions, and Applications. *Journal of Vocational Behavior, 65*, 14–38.

Furlong, A., & Cartmel, F. (2005). *Graduates from Disadvantaged Families: Early Labour Market Experiences*. Bristol: Joseph Rowntree Foundation.

Furlong, A., Cartmel, F., Biggart, A., Sweeting, H., & West, P. (2003). *Youth Transitions: Patterns of Vulnerability and Processes of Social Inclusion*. Edinburgh: Scottish Executive.

Furlong, A., Cartmel, F., & Biggart, A. (2006). Choice Biographies and Transitional Linearity: Re-conceptualising Modern Youth Transitions. *PAPERS Revista de Sociologia, 79*, 225–239.

Garsten, C., & Jacobsson, K. (2003). Learning to be Employable: An Introduction. In C. Garsten & K. Jacobsson (Eds.), *Learning to be Employable: New Agendas on Work, Responsibility and Learning in a Globalizing World*. London: Palgrave Macmillan.

Gazier, B. (2001). Employability: The Complexity of a Policy Notion. In P. Weinert, M. Baukens, P. Bollérot, M. Pineschi-Gapènne, & U. Walwei (Eds.), *Employability: From Theory to Practice* (pp. 3–23). London: Transaction Publishers.

Gibb, A. (2002). Creating Conducive Environments for Learning and Entrepreneurship: Living with, Dealing with, Creating and Enjoying Uncertainty and Complexity. *Industry and Higher Education, 16*(3), 135–148.

Giddens, A. (1991). *Modernity and Self-identity: Self and Society in the Late Modern Age*. Stanford: Stanford University Press.

Gunz, H. P., Evans, M. G., & Jalland, R. (2000). Career Boundaries in a 'Boundaryless' World. In M. A. Peiperl, M. B. Arthur, R. Goffee, & T. Morris (Eds.), *Career Frontiers: New Conceptions of Working Lives*. Oxford: Oxford University Press.

Hager, P. & Holland, S. (Eds.) (2006). *Graduate Attributes, Learning and Employability*. Dordrecht: Springer.

Hall, D. T. (2001). Careers in and Out of Organizations. In *Foundations for Organizational Science*. Thousand Oaks, London, and New Delhi: Sage.

Harvey, R. (2000). New Realities: the Relationship Between Higher Education and Employment. *Tertiary Education Management, 6*(1), 3–17.

Harvey, L. (2001). Defining and Measuring Employability. *Quality in Higher Education, 7*(2), 97–109.

Hassard, J., McCann, L., & Morris, J. L. (2008). *Managing in the New Economy: Restructuring White-Collar Work in the USA, UK and Japan.* Cambridge: Cambridge University Press.

Heelas, P., Lasch, S., & Morris, P. (Eds.). (1996). *Detraditionalisation.* Oxford: Blackwell.

Heery, E., & Noon, M. (2017). *Dictionary of Human Resource Management.* Oxford: Oxford University Press.

Henry, C., Hill, F., & Leicht, C. (2005). Entrepreneurship Education and Training: Can Entrepreneurship Be Taught? Part I. *Education & Training, 47*(2/3; Social Science Premium Collection), 98.

Hillage, J., & Pollard, E. (1998). *Employability: Developing a Framework for Policy Analysis.* London: Department for Education and Employment.

Holmes, L. (2001). Reconsidering Graduate Employability: The Graduate Identity Approach. *Quality in Higher Education, 7*(2), 111–120.

Holmes, L. (2011). Competing Perspectives on Graduate Employability: Possession, Position or Process?. *Studies in Higher Education, 38*(4), 538–554.

Huber, M., Brown, C., Hutchings, P., Gale, R., Miller, R., & Breen, M. (Eds.). (2007). *Integrative Learning: Opportunities to Connect. Public Report of the Integrative Learning Project.* Stanford, CA: the Association of American Colleges and Universities and The Carnegie Foundation for the Advancement of Teaching. Retrieved from http://gallery.carnegiefoundation.org/ilp/.

Huws U., Spencer, N. H., Syrdal, D. S., & Holts, K. (2017). *Work in the European Gig Economy.* Published by FEPS, UNI Europa and University of Hertfordshire.

ILO—International Labour Office. (2010). *Characterizing the School-to-Work Transitions of Young Men and Women: Evidence from the ILO School-to-Work Transition Surveys.* Employment working paper No. 51, Geneva: ILO.

ILO—International Labour Office. (2019). *World Employment and Social Outlook – Trends.* International Labour Office – Geneva: ILO.

Inkson, K., & Arthur, M. B. (2001). How to Be a Successful Career Capitalist. *Organizational Dynamics, 30*(1), 48–61.

Inkson, K., & Elkin, G. (2008). Landscape with Travelers: The Context of Careers in Developed Nations. In R. van Esbroeck & J. Athanasou (Eds.), *International Handbook of Career Guidance* (pp. 69–94). New York, NY: Springer.

Ipeirotis, P. G. (2010). *Demographics of Mechanical Turk.* CeDER Working Paper 10-01. New York: Stern School of Business, New York University.

Istituto Nazionale di Statistica (ISTAT) (2019). *Rapporto Annuale 2019. La situazione del Paese.* Rome: ISTAT.

Jackson, D. (2016). Re-Conceptualising Graduate Employability: The Importance of Pre-Professional Identity. *Higher Education Research & Development, 35*(5), 925–939.

Keep, E., & Mayhew, K. (2010). Moving Beyond Skills as a Social and Economic Panacea. *Work, Employment and Society, 24*(3), 565–577.

Klein, P. G., & Bullock, J. B. (2006). Can Entrepreneurship be Taught? *Journal of Agricultural and Applied Economics, 38*(2), 429–439.

Knight, P. T., & Yorke, M. (2003). *Assessment, Learning and Employability*. Maidenhead: Society for Research in Higher Education and the Open University Press.

Kolb, D. A. (1984). *Experiential Learning: Experience as the Source of Learning and Development*. Englewood Cliffs, N.J: Prentice-Hall.

Kolvereid, L. (1996). Organizational Employment Versus Self-Employment: Reasons for Career Choice Intentions. *Entrepreneurship Theory and Practice, 20*(3), 23–31.

Kolvereid, L. (2016). Preference for SELF-EMPLOYMENT: Prediction of New Business Start-Up Intentions and Efforts. *The International Journal of Entrepreneurship and Innovation, 17*(2), 100–109.

Kuttner, R. (2018). *Can Democracy Survive Global Capitalism?* New York: Norton&Company Inc.

Lave, J., & Wenger, E. (1991). *Situated Learning: Legitimate Peripheral Participation*. New York, NY: Cambridge University Press.

Lévi-Strauss, C. (1950). Introduction à l'oeuvre de Marcel Mauss. In *Mauss, Sociologie et Anthropologie*. Paris.

Leonard, D. (2000). Hagerdies: Competencies and Artistry. *Higher Education in Europe, 25*(2), 181–92.

Magnum, G. L. (1976). *Employability, Employment, and Income*. Saltlake City: Olympus.

Mason, G., Williams, G., & Cranmer, S. (2009). Employability Skills Initiatives in Higher Education: What Effects Do They Have on Graduate Labour Market Outcomes? *Education Economics, 17*(1), 1–30.

McGuinness, S. (2006). Overeducation and the Labour Market. *Journal of Economic Surveys, 20*, 3, Oxford: Blackwell Publishing Ltd.

McKinsey Global Institute. (2017). *Independent Work: Choice, Necessity, and the Gig Economy*. MGI Reports. Retrieved February, 2020, from https://www.mckinsey.com/featured-insights/employment-and-growth/independent-work-choice-necessity-and-the-gig-economy.

Mezirow, J. (1997). Transformative Learning: Theory to Practice. *New Directions for Adult and Continuing Education, 74*, 5–12.

Michoń, P. (2019). The Great Recession and the Youth Labour Market in European Countries: The Demographic Versus the Labour Market Effect. In *Youth Unemployment and Job Insecurity in Europe: Problems, Risk Factors and Policies*. London: Edward Elgar Publishing.

Moreland, N. (2006). Entrepreneurship & Higher Education: An Employability Perspective. In *Learning & employability Series*. York: ESECT.
Morley, L. (2001). Producing New Workers: Quality, Equality and Employability in Higher Education. *Quality in Higher Education, 7*, 2.
Morselli, D. (2019). *The Change Laboratory for Teacher Training in Entrepreneurship Education. A New Skills Agenda for Europe*. Cham: Springer Briefs in Education.
Muller, W., & Gangl, M. (2003). *Transitions from Education to Work in Europe*. New York: Oxford University Press.
Mwasalwiba, E. S. (2010). Entrepreneurship Education: A Review of Its Objectives, Teaching Methods, and Impact Indicators. *Education & Training, 52*(1), 20–47.
Neck, H. M., & Corbett, A. C. (2018). The Scholarship of Teaching and Learning Entrepreneurship. *Entrepreneurship Education and Pedagogy, 1*(1), 8–41.
O'Higgins, N. (2012). *This Time It's Different? Youth labour markets during 'The Great Recession'*. IZA discussion paper, No. 6434. Bonn: Institute for the Study of Labor.
OECD. (2000). *From Initial Education to Working Life: Making Transitions Work*. Paris: OECD.
OECD. (2017). *OECD Employment Outlook 2017: The Future of Work*. Paris: OECD Publishing.
OECD. (2019). *OECD Employment Outlook 2019: The Future of Work*. Paris: OECD Publishing.
Ortiz, L. (2010). Not the Right Job, But a Secure One: Over-Education and Temporary Employment in France, Italy and Spain. *Work, Employment and Society, 24*, 47–64.
Pesole, A., Urzí Brancati, M. C., Fernández-Macías, E., Biagi, F., & González Vázquez, I. (2018). *Platform Workers in Europe*. Luxembourg: Publications Office of the European Union.
Phillips, F., Yu, C., Hameed, T., & El Akhdary, M. A. (2017). The Knowledge Society's Origins and Current Trajectory. *International Journal of Innovation Studies, 1*, 175–191.
Purcell, K., & Elias, P. (2004). *Seven Years On: Graduate Careers in a Changing Labour Market*. Manchester: Higher Education Careers Services Unit.
Purcell, K., Morley, M., & Rowley, G. (2002). *Employers in the New Graduate Labour Market: Recruiting from a Wider Spectrum of Graduates*. London: CIHE-ESRU.
Purcell, K, Elias, P., Artfield, G., Behle, H., Ellison, R., & Luchinskaya, D. (2013). *Transitions Into Employment, Further Study and Other Outcomes*. The Futuretrack stage 4 Report. Manchester/Coventry: HECSU/Warwick Institute for Employment Research.

Rae, D. (2004). Practical Theories from Entrepreneurs' Stories: Discursive Approaches to Entrepreneurial Learning. *Journal of Small Business and Enterprise Development, 11*(2), 195–202.

Rae, D. (2007). Connecting Enterprise and Graduate Employability: Challenges to the Higher Education Culture and Curriculum? *Education + Training, 49*(8/9), 605–619.

Raffe, D. (2011). Cross-National Differences in Education-Work Transitions. In M. London (Ed.), *The Oxford Handbook of Lifelong Learning* (pp. 312–328). New York: Oxford University Press.

Ranga, M., & Etzkowitz, H. (2013). Triple Helix Systems: An Analytical Framework for Innovation Policy and Practice in the Knowledge Society. *Industry and Higher Education, 27*(4), 237–262.

Roper, J., Ganesh, I., & Inkson, K. (2010). Neoliberalism and Knowledge Interests in Boundaryless Careers Discourse. *Work, Employment and Society, 24*(4), 661–679.

Rothwell, A., & Rothwell, F. (2017). Graduate Employability: A Critical Oversight. In M. Tomlinson & L. Holmes (Eds.), *Graduate Employability in Context.* London: Palgrave Macmillan.

Saxenian, A. (1994). *Regional Advantage: Culture and Competition in Silicon Valley and Route 128.* Boston: Harvard University Press.

Scott, P. (1995). *The Meanings of Mass Higher Education.* Buckingham: SRHE/Open University Press.

Serrano Pascual, A. (2001). The Role of Social and Civil Partnership Networks in Combating Youth Unemployment. In A. Serrano Pascual (Ed.), *Enhancing Youth Employability Through Social and Civil Partnerships* (pp. 13–60). Brussels: European Trade Union Institute.

Sewell, P., & Dacre Pool, L. (2010). Moving from Conceptual Ambiguity to Operational Clarity: Employability, Enterprise and Entrepreneurship in Higher Education. *Education + Training, 52*(1), 89–94.

Sin, C., & Neave, G. (2016). Employability Deconstructed: Perceptions of Bologna Stakeholders. *Studies in Higher Education, 41*(8), 1447–1462.

Slade, A. (2014). *Mind the Soft Skills Gap.* Association for Talent Development. Retrieved from online: www.td.org/Publications/Magazines/TD/TD-Archive/2014/04/Intelligence-Mind-the-Soft-Skills-Gap.

Steur, J., Jansen, E., & Hofman, A. (2016). Towards Graduateness: Exploring Academic Intellectual Development in University Master's Students. *Educational Research and Evaluation, 22*(1–2), 6–22.

Stewart, T. A. (2001). *The Wealth of Knowledge.* London: Nicholas Brealey.

Suleman, F. (2016, June 21–23). *Employability Skills of Higher Education Graduates: Little Consensus on a Much-Discussed Subject.* 2nd International Conference on Higher Education Advances, HEAd'16, Valencia, Spain.

Sullivan, S. E., & Arthur, M. B. (2006). The Evolution of the Boundaryless Career Concept: Examining Physical and Psychological Mobility. *Journal of Vocational Behavior, 69*, 19–29.

Thijssen, J. G. L., Van der Heijden, B. I. J. M., & Rocco, T. S. (2008). Toward the Employability–Link Model: Current Employment Transition to Future Employment Perspectives. *Human Resource Development Review, 7*(2), 165–183.

Tomlinson, M. (2008). 'The Degree Is Not Enough': Students' Perceptions of the Role of Higher Education Credentials for Graduate Work and Employability. *British Journal of Sociology of Education, 29*(1), 49–61.

Tomlinson, M. (2013). *Education, Work and Identity*. London: Bloomsbury.

Tomlinson, M. (2017). Forms of Graduate Capital and Their Relationship to Graduate Employability. *Education + Training, 59*(4), 338–352.

Tomlinson, M., & Holmes, L. (2017). *Graduate Employability in Context: Theory, Research and Debate*. Basingstoke: Palgrave Macmillan.

U.S. Department of Education (2013). *Employability Skills Framework*. https://cte.ed.gov/initiatives/employability-skills-framework

Van Dam, K. (2004). Antecedents and Consequences of Employability Orientation. *European Journal of Work and Organizational Psychology, 13*, 29–51.

Van der Heijde, C. M., & Van der Heijden, B. I. J. M. (2006). A Competence-Based and Multidimensional Operationalization and Measurement of Employability. *Human Resource Management, 45*(3), 449–476.

Verd, J. M., Barranco, O., & Bolíbar, M. (2019). Youth Unemployment and Employment Trajectories in Spain During the Great Recession: What Are the Determinants? *Journal for Labour Market Research, 53*(4), 1–20.

Wang, C. L., & Chugh, H. (2014). Entrepreneurial Learning: Past Research and Future Challenges. *International Journal of Management Reviews, 1*, 24.

Wesley, S., Jackson, V., & Lee, M. (2017). The Perceived Importance of Core Soft Skills Between Retailing and Tourism Management Students, Faculty and Businesses. *Employee Relations, 39*(1), 79–99.

Williams, S., Dodd, L. J., Steele, C., & Randall, R. (2016). A Systematic Review of Current Understandings of Employability. *Journal of Education and Work, 29*(8), 877–901.

Wyn, J., & White, R. (1997). *Rethinking Youth*. London: Sage.

Yorke, M. (2004). *Employability in Higher Education: What It Is—What It Is Not*. York: Higher Education Academy/ESECT.

Yorke, M., & Knight, P. (2006). *Embedding Employability Into the Curriculum*. York: Higher Education Academy Learning Series.

CHAPTER 2

Policies and Practices in European Regional Development

Abstract This chapter provides an overview of the key policies and strategies that are directly linked to regional development and universities. After a summary on how regional policies have changed over time, it outlines educational policies affecting higher education, then offers an overview of global goals, which are, or should be, the overarching framework for policy interventions at all levels. The chapter concludes with some considerations about the implications of graduate employability's theme in regional economies and local markets.

Keywords Regional development • Educational policies • Sustainable development goals • Smart specialisation • Policy alignment

2.1 Regional Policies

The regional investment policy of the European Union, also known as the Cohesion Policy, aims to reduce regional disparities in income, wealth, and opportunities. It originated in the Treaty of Rome (1957), which established the Economic Community. In 1968, the Directorate-General for Regional Policy of the European Commission was created, and today the DG for Regional and Urban Policy (the DG REGIO, as it is now called) manages investment policy at the regional level. Investments aimed at supporting job creation, competitiveness, economic growth, improved quality of life, and sustainable development are made through financial

G. Paviotti, *'Regional Universities' and Pedagogy*,
https://doi.org/10.1007/978-3-030-53680-0_2

instruments of the European Regional Development Fund (ERDF), the European Social Fund (ESF), and the Cohesion Fund (CF). The EARDF, created in 1975, provides funds for investments for companies, infrastructure, capital risk, and local development, and furnishes technical assistance for the implementation of these funds. The ESF, which has been in place since the Treaty of Rome, is tasked with integrating working life, and provides funds for employment and particularly training. Both funds are allocated at the regional level. Instead, at the member nation level, the CF, created in 1994, finances transport and infrastructure projects.

The regional policy is further implemented through the Common Agricultural Policy (CAP), which has as financial instruments the European Agricultural Guarantee Fund (EAGF established in 2005), the European Agricultural Fund for Rural Development (EAFRD established in 2005), and the European fisheries fund (EFF established in 2006).

The main purpose of the Cohesion Policy is to harmonise regions and avoid disparities, and over a third of the European Union budget is allocated to this goal. As regards regional intervention in educational policies within the CP, the European Social Fund is the most interesting instrument. It should be noted that the ESF is managed by the Directorate-General of Labour, while educational policies depend on the Directorate-General for Education and Training. According to the analysis carried out by Tomé (2013), the ESF had four identifiable phases connected with the economic performance and labour market of the European Union over time: the first phase (1958–1970) was focused on the unemployed; the second phase (1972–1983) on the labour market, including production sectors (e.g. textile, agriculture); the third phase (1984–1989), or "transitional phase," that did not present major changes; and the fourth (1990 onwards) on the overall regional objective of competitiveness and growth. Now, the ESF continues the goals of the fourth phase, addressing multiple targets according to regional needs, including work to assist higher education in meeting the overall perceived need of highly skilled workers, by "helping universities and vocational training institutions to build closer relations with businesses and employers in their countries and regions—such that graduates can move smoothly from learning into employment. University postgraduate research and development is supported by ESF funds to increase the number of young entrepreneurs and innovators, particularly in high-technology sectors" (website of the European Social Fund[1]).

The most significant new effort of recent years to foster CP goals at regional levels has been the establishment of the Smart Specialisation Strategy (S3, better known as RIS3, research and innovation strategies for smart specialisation). "Smart specialisation" was first articulated by academics (Foray et al. 2009), then adopted by policymakers (Fotakis et al. 2014) and defined in Regulation (EU) N° 1303/2013 of the European Parliament and of the Council as follows:

> "Smart specialisation strategy" means the national or regional innovation strategies which set priorities in order to build competitive advantage by developing and matching research and innovation own strengths to business needs in order to address emerging opportunities and market developments in a coherent manner, while avoiding duplication and fragmentation of efforts; a smart specialisation strategy may take the form of, or be included in, a national or regional research and innovation (R&I) strategic policy framework.

Important RIS3 features that improve on previous policies include (a) a non-neutral policy that focuses on specific domains; (b) participation and contribution from stakeholders, including universities, through the entrepreneurial discovery process,[2] and (c) an attempt to relate research and innovation resources with the economic features of the place (Foray and Goenaga 2013). The greatest contribution of the RIS3 for the programming period 2014–2020 has been the implementation of "ex-ante conditionality": access to Structural Funds for RIS3 Thematic Objective 1 (strengthening research, technological development, and innovation) is conditioned on the drafting of national and regional specialisation strategies. Thus Regions, including less developed ones, should begin processes of innovation at the regional level. Some authors point out, however, that this does not necessarily mean that the process will be actually carried out, and the objectives will be achieved (Hassink and Gong 2019).

2.2 Educational Policies

The European Union does not have direct legislative powers over higher education. Rather, its policy on education and training is designed to support the action of the Member States and address common challenges (European Commission website). Therefore, all Joint Declarations or Strategies should be signed by Ministers of the Member States to enter into force, and are then implemented through national laws and regulations issued by national governments.

Higher-education policies in past decades have been strongly shaped by the issue of employability, with policies on the "societal" or "regional" role of the university, or "university-business cooperation". Beginning with the 1998 Sorbonne Declaration,[3] "employability" has been one of the key objectives for the realisation of the European Higher Education Area following the Bologna Declaration (June 1999).[4] This focus articulated to some extent the already progressing shift of universities from a mission of civic development and liberal education of citizens to a more active role in answering economic needs (Sin and Neave 2016; Tomusk 2004).

The relation between university and business has been widely studied within the University-Business Cooperation (UBC) concept, which includes, though does not directly address, employability. Since the mid-twentieth century and before the signing of the Bologna Declaration, in Europe overall there has been a shift towards a more societal role of universities (Goddard 2009; Zomer and Benneworth 2011), which includes special attention to links with business. The concept and fundamentals of the "Third Mission" of universities have been widely discussed and questioned, though its definition remains unclear, except as a "residual term, encompassing all university activities not covered by the first two missions of teaching and research" (E3M 2010). Most definitions of the Third Mission include:

- Knowledge and other university capabilities outside academic environments (Molas-Gallart et al. 2002) that refer to the Third Stream of universities.
- Social, enterprising, innovation activities that universities carry out alongside their teaching and research activities whereby additional benefits are created for society (Montesinos et al. 2008).
- Activities of the universities that stimulate and direct the application and exploitation of knowledge to the benefit of the social, cultural, and economic development of our society (HEFCW 2004).

Up to the second half of the twentieth century, the UBC discourse tended to be centred around the exploitation of research, based on the dominant paradigm of a technology push, undermining the role played in innovation by other disciplines, such as arts, humanities, and social sciences (European Commission 2011). The "triple helix" approach (Etzkowitz 2008) and its developments (Ranga and Etzkowitz 2013), which emphasise innovation as the result of the links between university, industry, and government, have additionally refined the university position as a key player within a territorial system.

A push forward has been the addition of a strong regional dimension to policies: "countries which wish to mobilise their higher education system or part of it in support of regional development, need to ensure that the higher education policy which embraces teaching, research and third task activities include an explicit regional dimension" (OECD 2007, p. 17). In 2011, the European Commission adopted the Agenda for the modernisation of Europe's higher-education system, inviting the Member States to promote "the systematic involvement of higher education institutions in the development of integrated local and regional development plans, and target regional support towards higher education-business cooperation particularly for the creation of regional hubs of excellence and specialisation" (European Commission 2011a). The European 2020 Growth Strategy, and in particular the Smart Specialisation Strategy, gives a significant role to higher-education institutions; its guide, "Connecting Universities to Regional Growth" (European Commission 2011), "seeks to ensure that universities are not excluded from (or chose not to engage with) the shaping of regional innovation strategies" (Goddard et al. 2013).

Trippl et al. (2015), and further completed by Kempton (2019), conceptualise at least four models of the university within a regional system:

- The entrepreneurial university (Etzkowitz 1983 and following developments): this model is based on the concept of the triple helix (business, policymakers, and academia) jointly working for economic growth and development. The university contribution mostly entails research innovation, patents, and spin-offs. The limit of this approach is the moderate extent to which it affects the regional dimension. It applies very easily to knowledge-intensive districts;
- The regional innovation system approach (Cooke et al. 2004), which focuses on the role of universities as bridges in the innovation-production process at the regional level, where knowledge transfer is one of the key activities. However, the approach does not consider how much knowledge comes from outside the region and contributes to the same goals;

- Mode 2 knowledge production (Gibbons et al. 1994) points out the emerging type of knowledge produced by universities, that, unlike linear and disciplinary forms, is generated by interactions between disciplines and is applicable to societal challenges. It refers to the concept of co-creation of knowledge (Trencher et al. 2014; Rinaldi et al. 2018). This approach has been criticised for neglecting "institutions, systems, natural eco-systems and the environment" (Trippl et al. 2015, p. 1726);
- The engaged university (Gunasekara 2006; Uyarra 2010). This model refers to the capability of the university to provide answers to regional needs, such as providing skills to students according to needs expressed by the territory, managing regional innovation networks, and so on. This approach, which is very region-based, tends to downplay the fact that universities are usually nationally established and obey national laws (for example, laws that define programs of study), and thus are not well poised to respond quickly to multiple regional needs;
- The civic university (Goddard 2009; Goddard et al. 2013) pays more attention to internal management and leadership that lead or hinder engagement with the outside world. This approach, however, has little explicit focus on the regional dimension, having principles that are mostly "spatially blind", with "limited evidence of success in practice" (Kempton 2019, p. 4).

Of interest in this context is HEInnovate, developed by the European Commission and the OECD, as "a self-assessment tool for Higher Education Institutions who wish to explore their innovative potential [...] through a process of identification, prioritisation and action planning in eight key areas": (1) leadership and governance; (2) organisational capacity; (3) entrepreneurial teaching and learning; (4) preparing and supporting entrepreneurs; (5) digital transformation and capability; (6) knowledge exchange and collaboration; (7) the internationalised institution; and (8) measuring impact (https://heinnovate.eu/en). Based on the concept of the entrepreneurial university, HEInnovate also incorporates further developments beyond the original concept. It does not directly address employability, but recent statements clarify that universities should be responsible for enhancing graduate employability and educating enterprising individuals (HEInnovate concept, June 2018). All these aspects include elements that together are expected to foster an entrepreneurial mindset, an asset in any kind of employment (Moreland 2006).

Overall, discourse about "regionalisation" of universities focuses on development and growth, as regional development is obviously linked with economic production and job creation. However, this involves domains that refer not only to the third university mission of "social, enterprising, innovation activities" for the benefit of society through relations with business, or to the second mission of research, but also to the first mission of teaching and learning. Thus there is a call for universities not merely to contribute to the required change, but to alter their very nature. For example, the demand for changes to the curriculum to meet the primary goal of training professionals able to serve economic needs (which seem to be mostly business needs rather than overarching societal needs) could undermine the long-standing traditional understanding of the first mission of teaching to form the educated citizens who are essential for the flourishing of democracy. This will be discussed more in-depth in Chap. 4, but should be kept in mind to understand the implications of relations between the macro- and meso-levels.

2.3 Global Goals

Participants in the United Nations Conference on Sustainable Development in Rio de Janeiro in 2012 defined a set of universal goals to meet the world's urgent environmental, political, and economic challenges. The Sustainable Development Goals (SDGs), also known as the Global Goals, with the horizon of the year 2030 (Agenda 2030[5]), were adopted by all United Nations Member States in 2015 and entered into force in January 2016. The 17 SDGs set 169 targets, which are "integrated and indivisible" (art. 18 of the Agenda), and commit States "to achieving sustainable development in its three dimensions—economic, social and environmental—in a balanced and integrated manner" (art. 2). Involvement and commitment of business together with policymakers and civil society are noted in art. 41: "We acknowledge the role of the diverse private sector, ranging from micro-enterprises to cooperatives to multinationals". It is no coincidence that the word "partnership" is reiterated throughout the document and is itself a goal (Goal 17. Strengthen the means of implementation and revitalise the global partnership for sustainable development). Partnership is obviously intended as a condition for the achievement of the goals globally between countries, as well as within defined geographical areas, and thus in a range of very different levels of development, from low-income to highly industrialised countries.

Among these deeply interrelated goals, two directly mention education and employment, and two focus further on regional development and rural/urban issues. Education and employment are the subjects of Goal 4: "Ensure inclusive and equitable quality education and promote lifelong learning opportunities for all" and Goal 8: "Promote sustained, inclusive and sustainable economic growth, full and productive employment and decent work for all". Regional development, particularly rural and urban issues, is articulated in Goal 11: "Make cities and human settlements inclusive, safe, resilient and sustainable" and to a lesser extent Goal 2: "End hunger, achieve food security and improved nutrition and promote sustainable agriculture" (referring in particular to target 2.3[6]).

The previous global goal initiative (Millennium Development Goals) was more focused on poverty alleviation, and the private sector was not asked to take direct responsibility, as it is in the SDGs. On the contrary, business is a particularly significant player in the SDGs framework. Mawdsley et al. (2013) defined this as a paradigm shift "from a post-aid world to development" to support growth and reduce inequalities. The main concept had already been aptly summarised by the OECD in 2011: "We recognise the central role of the private sector in advancing innovation, creating wealth, income and jobs, mobilising domestic resources and in turn contributing to poverty reduction". In fact, the private sector, mostly represented by large international companies based in Western countries (Scheyvens et al. 2016), was involved in high-level political forums to define the SDGs. The new approach was met with concern by many researchers and experts. Scheyvens et al. (2016, pp. 376–380) identified at least six barriers to full deployment of capacities of the private sector. First, they objected to the neoliberal agenda promoted by the large Western international companies who helped define the SDGs, and yet who were partly responsible for creating in the first place the very problems that the SDGs were meant to ameliorate (Pingeot 2014, p. 23). Second, structural poverty is not addressed in the SDGs, particularly that found in the "enabling environments" in some countries, where the land is mostly in the hands of large corporations. Third, when involving business in a partnership to promote development needs, an accountable outcome must be borne in mind, and the important role of business in environmental and social degradation must not be ignored or understated.

Fourth, present business models are based on short-term and flexible arrangements, while higher goals require long-term vision. Fifth, human development is not the core business of the private sector, and any partnership must insist on goals of sustainability as well. Sixth, the primary goal of private business is profit: while some firms may have corporate social responsibility goals, often their competition does not. It is naive to think that even well-intentioned businesses will sacrifice necessary profit or even their survival for the broader interests of environmental and social sustainability. Many authors acknowledge that the private sector can contribute enormously to the achievement of SDG goals, but suggest that legislation should be passed "to oblige businesses to be more socially and environmentally responsible", therefore to be responsible and accountable for their actions. Spangenberg, in his critical assessment of the SDGs, reaches a similar conclusion, calling for re-regulation against deregulation (2016).

Discussion of education in the SDGs appears to be linked with the concept of growth. Higher education is included implicitly in all goals and targets referring to education, and explicitly in Goal target 4.3, to "ensure equal access for all women and men to affordable and quality technical, vocational, and tertiary education, including university". The Sustainable Development Solutions Network (SDSN) Guide entitled "Getting Started with the SDGs in Universities" (2017), the most comprehensive guidance provided so far, proposes an implementation pathway of three phases and five steps that, starting from mapping internal resources (Recognition phase, step 1), pass through capacity building and identification of priorities (Opportunities phase, steps 2 and 3), and conclude with a strategy for integrating, implementing, and embedding SDGs and monitoring and evaluating progress (Organising phase, steps 4 and 5). Overall, this process would include contributions from all the dimensions of the university:

- Teaching and learning, by integrating "education for sustainability" into all subjects, providing skills for implementing sustainable solutions, and promoting inclusive policies of access and retention.
- Research, by providing evidence-based knowledge, solutions, and technologies to the global community and economy through disciplinary, interdisciplinary, and transdisciplinary approaches, providing capacity building for developing countries and improving diversity in research.

- Organisational governance, by implementing the SDGs through operational policies encompassing also financing, support services, human resources management, and student administration.
- External leadership, by strengthening public engagement and participation in addressing the SDGs, facilitating cross dialogue, ensuring university representation, and supporting the design of sustainable policies.

The authors of the Guide recognise that the high degree of diversity among universities in many nations requires that the "engaged" universities have a high degree of autonomy in implementing the suggested steps.

UNESCO has also contributed to pursuing global goals for sustainable development through education. Its 2015 "Guidelines on sustainability science in research and education" and 2017 "Practical guidelines to apply sustainability science frameworks: science-policy-society interface policy paper" support universities in pursuing overall sustainability, with special focus on environmental sustainability.

The guideline suggestions on how to effectively integrate education for sustainability at all levels have met with challenges to specific aspects, such as curriculum (Leal Filho 2018), transdisciplinarity (Steinfeld and Mino 2009), and stakeholder relations and contributions (García-González et al. 2017), but more generally, major concerns have been raised about the role that the guidelines proposed for the university. Some question the predominance of technology and hard sciences over humanities and social sciences (Boni et al. 2016). Others take issue with the proposition that the university serves society by fostering development in only one (neoliberal) way (Stein et al. 2016).

Finally, even if regional development is already included in the concept of partnership for both dimensions already analysed, it is worth focusing on Goal 11, to "Make cities and human settlements inclusive, safe, resilient and sustainable". This goal is articulated into six targets to be achieved by 2030 and four additional general targets with no achievement deadline. It should be stressed again that the SDGs are global goals that cover issues not necessarily applicable, or applicable to a lesser degree, to Europe. For the purpose of this chapter, attention should be paid in particular to targets related to transport (11.2), sustainable human settings (11.3 and 11.b), and in particular "economic, social and environmental links between urban, peri-urban and rural areas by strengthening national and regional development planning" (11.a). Rural areas make up about half of the

European Union territory, and according to 2015 Eurostat demographics, 28.0% of the EU-28 population lived in a rural area, while 40.4% lived in cities and the rest (31.6%) in towns and suburbs. In the years 2010–2015, the population in rural areas increased by 1.7% and was mainly elderly (OECD statistics 2018[7]). In terms of tertiary education, there was a gap of more than 20% between rural dwellers and city inhabitants (age: 30–34). These few figures already give an overview of how the population is distributed across national territories, particularly highly educated citizens. Granted that Goal 11 relates to sustainability overall, and does not develop the concept of "regional development", one nonetheless wonders how development and innovation can be achieved in rural areas inhabited by a predominantly older and low-skilled population and how skilled young workers can be attracted here, rather than to urban areas.

2.4 Towards Sustainable Growth: Overall Goals and a Missed Policy Alignment

It should be acknowledged that the neoliberal view provides the overarching framework in which all policies and global goals are designed and (tentatively) implemented: business is considered the driving force of social, economic, and environmental development towards the primary objective of growth. In this sense, it can be said that the macro-level of policies is definitely aligned. It seems that alternatives are not considered, and that "dissonant voices" fail to emerge, at least among policymakers.

However, in spite of this choral position, it seems that there is still some policy misalignment among levels of implementation. The first reason is the number of administrative and policy levels: super-national, national, regional, and, in some cases, provincial. For example, the definition of a smart specialisation strategy is a necessary condition for receiving funding from the European Union for research and innovation. However, the national government first defines national priorities, which are then deployed into regional priorities that often depend on choices made by regional governments. The level of development of regions is the most critical point identified by research: more developed regions tend to have more success in obtaining EU funding for programmes to promote sustainable growth. Less developed regions usually lack highly trained planners and policymakers adept in long-term planning for development. Sometimes a smart specialisation strategy can be cobbled together by overburdened regional officials just because it is a requirement for obtaining funds, and not as the result of a thorough analysis of results of a participatory "bottom-up" discovery process that truly represents the reality of the region's needs and potential. Given this discrepancy between regions, some doubts can be raised about the implementation of the entrepreneurial discovery process and interpretation of results for policy planning. In addition, in less developed regions, manufacturing usually predominates: these businesses are not marked by significant research and development, and thus innovation, and their contributions to innovative programmes, can be limited (Novotný et al. 2016; Vallance et al. 2018).

In addition, regional governments might answer more to the immediate practical needs of local residents, for example, for more jobs, and may not take a long-term perspective on growth through innovation and sustainable practices. Also, regions should ideally carry out stakeholder analysis for participatory processes by involving all representatives of stakes, but there is a real risk that only dominant social groups that regularly collaborate with governments are invited to participate (Grillitsch 2016).

The smart specialisation strategy at the regional level counts on the capabilities of local universities. Clearly, universities vary, and some may be more teaching-based, others more research-based, some more devoted to liberal arts, and others to STEM disciplines. These institutions have global, national, and local dimensions. Various models have been proposed for universities to serve regional development as active agents in a global-regional innovation system. Uyarra's (2010) analysis of the regional role of universities identified several contradictions. Universities should act regionally, but are evaluated at a national level according to different metrics. They are expected to influence policy, transfer knowledge, provide adequate human resources through teaching, and conduct research through partnership. Thus they manage a complex and multi-level agenda, of which "economic development duty" is only one issue. The idea that any university can perform such a complex role in any regional territory belies a "one-size-fits-all" approach, not a genuine place-based approach. Also, it is not necessarily the case that research specialisations of the institution line up with regional economic needs. Graduate employment also plays a role within this picture: in an "ideal" developmental line, graduates offer competencies that promote the prosperity of the region where they choose to live or where the university is located. However, if we consider prosperity driven by business needs or local economies based on low-skilled industries, there would be many "doomed" disciplines because they are not deemed "useful" for business. It can be hoped that an overall cultural shift will see global goals integrated into the responsibility of individual citizens and corporate social responsibility, but at present, this seems not to be embedded in our society, and most probably the flow of graduates to urban centres or to more developed regions will continue.

Notes

1. https://ec.europa.eu/esf/main.jsp?catId=51&langId=en.
2. The entrepreneurial discovery process is "a process in which participants from different environments (policy, business, academia, etc.) are discovering and producing information about potential new activities, identifying potential opportunities that emerge through this interaction, while policymakers assess outcomes and ways to facilitate the realisation of this potential" (Smart Specialization Platform, retrieved April 2020).
3. "We hereby commit ourselves to encouraging a common frame of reference, aimed at improving external recognition and facilitating student mobility as well as employability", Sorbonne Declaration 1998. This declaration was signed by the ministries of France, Germany, Italy, and United Kingdom.
4. "Adoption of a system of easily readable and comparable degrees, also through the implementation of the Diploma Supplement, in order to promote European citizens employability and the international competitiveness of the European higher education system". The Bologna declaration was signed by 29 Ministries of Education, and to date, 47 countries have joined the Bologna process.
5. "Transforming our world: the 2030 Agenda for Sustainable Development", https://sustainabledevelopment.un.org/post2015/transformingourworld.
6. 2.3 By 2030, double the agricultural productivity and incomes of small-scale food producers, in particular women, indigenous peoples, family farmers, pastoralists and fishers, including through secure and equal access to land, other productive resources and inputs, knowledge, financial services, markets and opportunities for value addition and non-farm employment.
7. https://data.oecd.org/popregion/national-area-distribution.htm.

References

Boni, A., Lopez-Fogues, A., & Walker, M. (2016). Higher Education and the Post-2015 Agenda: A Contribution from the Human Development Approach. *Journal of Global Ethics, 12*(1), 17–28.

Cooke, P., Heidenreich, M., & Braczyk, H.-J. (Eds.). (2004). *Regional Innovation Systems* (2nd ed.). London: Routledge.

E3M Consortium. (2010). *Needs and Constraints Analysis of the Three Dimensions of Third Mission Activities*. Retrieved from http://e3mproject.eu/Three-dim-third-mission-act.pdf.

Etzkowitz, H. (1983). Entrepreneurial Scientists and Entrepreneurial Universities in American Academic Science. *Minerva, 21*(2), 198–233.

Etzkowitz, H. (2008). *The Triple Helix: University–Industry–Government Innovation In Action*. London: Routledge.

European Commission. (2011). *Connecting Universities to Regional Growth: A Practical Guide*. DG Regio.

European Commission. (2011a). *Communication from the Commission to the European Parliament, the Council, the European Economic and Social Committee and the Committee of the Regions*. Supporting Growth and Jobs—An Agenda for the Modernisation of Europe's Higher Education Systems, Brussels, 20.9.2011 COM(2011) 567 Final.

Foray, D., & Goenaga, X. (2013). *The Goals of Smart Specialisation*. S3 Policy Brief 01/2013, JRC-IPTS, Seville.

Foray, D., David, P., & Hall, B. (2009). *Smart Specialisation—The Concept*. Knowledge Economists, Policy Brief 9.

Fotakis, C., Rosenmöller, M., Brennan, J., Matei, L., Nikolov, R., Petitot, C., & Puukka, J. (2014). *The Role of Universities and Research Organisations as Drivers for Smart Specialisation at Regional Level*. Luxembourg: European Commission.

García-González, E., Jiménez-Fontana, R., Azcárate Goded, P., & Cardeñoso, J. M. (2017). Inclusion of Sustainability in University Classrooms Through Methodology. In *Handbook of Theory and Practice of Sustainable Development in Higher Education*. Cham: Springer.

Gibbons, M., Limoges, C., Nowotny, H., Schwartzman, S., Scott, P., & Trow, M. (1994). *The New Production of Knowledge: The Dynamics of Science and Research in Contemporary Societies*. London: Sage.

Goddard, J. (2009). *Re-Inventing the Civic University*. London: NESTA.

Goddard, J., Kempton, L., & Vallance, P. (2013). The Civic University: Connecting the Global and the Local. In R. Cappello, A. Olechnicka, & G. Gorzelak (Eds.), *Universities, Cities and Regions, Loci for Knowledge and Innovation Creation* (pp. 43–63). London: Routledge.

Grillitsch, M. (2016). Institutions, Smart Specialisation Dynamics and Policy. *Environment and Planning C: Government and Policy, 34*, 22–37.

Gunasekara, C. (2006). Reframing the Role of Universities in the Development of Regional Innovation Systems. *Journal of Technology Transfer, 31*(1), 101–113.

Hassink, R., & Gong, H. (2019). Six Critical Questions About Smart Specialization. *European Planning Studies, 27*(10), 2049–2065.

HEFCW. (2004). *Future Third Mission Funding Arrangements in Wales*. HEFCW.

HEINNOVATE. (2018). *Concept Note. The Entrepreneurial and Innovative Higher Education Institution*. A Review of the Concept and Its Relevance Today. Retrieved from https://heinnovate.eu/sites/default/files/heinnovate_concept_note.pdf.

Kempton, L. (2019). Wishful Thinking? Towards a More Realistic Role for Universities in Regional Innovation Policy. *European Planning Studies, 27*(11), 2248–2265.

Leal Filho, W. (Ed.). (2018). *Implementing Sustainability in the Curriculum of Universities. Approaches, Methods and Projects*. World Sustainability Series, Springer International Publishing.

Mawdsley, E., Savage, L., & Kim, S.-M. (2013). A "Post-Aid World"? Paradigm Shift in Foreign Aid and Development Cooperation at the 2011 Busan High-Level Forum. *The Geographical Journal, 180*(1), 27–38.

Molas-Gallart, J., Salter, A., Patel, P., Scott, A., & Duran, X. (2002). *Measuring Third Stream Activities. Final Report to the Russell Group of Universities*. Brighton: SPRU, University of Sussex.

Montesinos, P., Carot, J. M., Martinez, J., & Mora, F. (2008). Third Mission Ranking for World Class Universities: Beyond Teaching and Research. *Higher Education in Europe, 33*(2–3), 259–271.

Moreland, N. (2006). Entrepreneurship & Higher Education: An Employability Perspective. In *Learning & Employability Series*. York: ESECT.

Novotný, J., Blažek, J., & Květoň, V. (2016). The Anatomy of Difference: Comprehending the Evolutionary Dynamics of Economic and Spatial Structure in the Austrian and Czech Economies. *European Planning Studies, 24*(4), 788–808.

OECD (Organisation for Economic Co-operation and Development). (2007). *Higher Education and Regions: Globally Competitive, Locally Engaged*. Paris: Organisation for Economic Cooperation and Development.

Pingeot, L. (2014). *Corporate Influence in the Post-15 Process*. Brot für die Welt Working Paper. Retrieved from https://www.brot-fuer-die-welt.de/fileadmin/mediapool/2_Downloads/Fachinformationen/Sonstiges/Corporate_influence_in_the_post_2015_process.pdf.

Ranga, M., & Etzkowitz, H. (2013). Triple Helix Systems: An Analytical Framework for Innovation Policy and Practice in the Knowledge Society. *Industry and Higher Education, 27*(4), 237–262.

Rinaldi, C., Cavicchi, A., Spigarelli, F., Lacchè, L., & Rubens, A. (2018). Universities and Smart Specialisation Strategy: From Third Mission to Sustainable Development Co-Creation. *International Journal of Sustainability in Higher Education, 19*(1), 67–84.

Scheyvens, R., Banks, G., & Hughes, E. (2016). The Private Sector and the SDGs: The Need to Move Beyond 'Business as Usual'. *Sustainable Development, 24*, 371–382.

SDSN Australia/Pacific. (2017). *Getting Started with the SDGs in Universities: A Guide for Universities, Higher Education Institutions, and the Academic Sector.* Melbourne: Australia, New Zealand and Pacific Edition. Sustainable Development Solutions Network—Australia/Pacific.

Sin, C., & Neave, G. (2016). Employability Deconstructed: Perceptions of Bologna Stakeholders. *Studies in Higher Education, 41*(8), 1447–1462.

Spangenberg, J. H. (2016). Hot Air or Comprehensive Progress? A Critical Assessment of the SDGs. *Sustainable Development, 25*(4), 311–321.

Stein, S., Andreotti, V. D. O., & Suša, R. (2016). 'Beyond 2015', Within the Modern/Colonial Global Imaginary? Global Development and Higher Education. *Critical Studies in Education, 60*(3), 281–301.

Steinfeld, J. I., & Mino, T. (2009). Education for Sustainable Development: The Challenge of Trans-Disciplinarity. *Sustain Sci, 4*(1), 1.

Tomé, E. (2013). The European Social Fund: A Very Specific Case Instrument of HRD Policy. *European Journal of Training and Development, 37*(4), 336–356.

Tomusk, V. (2004). Three BOLOGNAS and a Pizza Pie: Notes on Institutionalization of the European Higher Education System. *International Studies in Sociology of Education, 14*(1), 75–96.

Trencher, G., Yarime, M., McCormick, K. B., Doll, C. N., & Kraines, S. B. (2014). Beyond the Third Mission: Exploring the Emerging University Function of Co-creation for Sustainability. *Science and Public Policy, 41*(2), 151–179.

Trippl, M., Sinozic, T., & Lawton Smith, H. (2015). The Role of Universities in Regional Development: Conceptual Models and Policy Institutions in the UK, Sweden and Austria. *European Planning Studies, 23*(9), 1722–1740.

Uyarra, E. (2010). Conceptualizing the Regional Roles of Universities, Implications and Contradictions. *European Planning Studies, 18*(8), 1227–1246.

Vallance, P., Blažek, J., Edwards, J., & Květŏn, V. (2018). Smart Specialisation in Regions with Less-Developed Research and Innovation Systems: A Changing Role for Universities? *Environment and Planning C: Politics and Space, 36*(2), 219–238.

Zomer, A., & Benneworth, P. (2011). The Rise of the University's Third Mission. In J. Enders, H. F. de Boer, & D. Westerheijden (Eds.), *Reform of Higher Education in Europe*. Rotterdam: Sense Publishers.

CHAPTER 3

Rural Territories and Graduate Employment

Abstract Employability should be assessed in terms of the features of labour markets, primarily determined by place-based economies. For example, the labour market works differently in wealthy countries than in countries struggling with low production and poor economies or in a state-based economy compared with a liberal economy. Within the same countries, or even at smaller administrative levels, such as the regions, differences can also be very significant. This chapter focuses on the characteristics of economy in rural areas, and the consequences for graduate employment.

Keywords Rural economies • Rural employment • Job seeking

3.1 Defining Rural

The term "rural" has never found a precise definition. According to Whitaker (1982), it was used the first time by the US Bureau of the Census in 1874 to define the population living outside of cities and towns with 8000 or more inhabitants. In general, the meaning of "rural" is defined by determining what it is not. The most precise definition of rural comes from statistical sources. In 1991 the European Commission proposed adopting the "degree of urbanisation" as a basis for statistics, distinguishing three types of area—densely populated, intermediate, and thinly

G. Paviotti, *Regional Universities' and Pedagogy*,
https://doi.org/10.1007/978-3-030-53680-0_3

populated (Dijkstra and Poelman 2014)[1]—based on population size, density, and contiguity to municipalities (administrative levels defined in the LAU2 document).[2] In 2014, classification based on 1 km^2 grid-cells was introduced to define density in contiguous sets of local areas, leading to the following definition (Eurostat glossary): "a rural area is an area where more than 50% of its population lives in rural grid cells".[3] Today, 57% of the European territory and 24% of its population are classified as rural (Eurostat 2017).

The definition is important not only for statistics about demographics: policies and investments are based on the distinction between rural and urban territories, as, for example, the Rural Development Policy of the European Commission,[4] and corresponding national rural development programmes.

The distinction between urban and rural has been criticised because it does not take into consideration the increased links and market exchanges between the two enabled by technology (Garrett 2005), or recognise the existence of in-between areas (Alexander Wandl et al. 2014). In 2018, the OECD published the "Rural 3.0" framework for rural development, which still refers to a clear distinction between urban and rural.[5] In short, the proposal suggests (OECD 2018):

- To shift from subsidising poorly productive activities to making strategic investments in more productive activities;
- To focus on local specificities to generate competitive advantages (e.g. local products);
- To address framework conditions (e.g. semi-public goods) which support enterprises indirectly;
- To improve coordination of policies from local to national and beyond;
- To decentralise policy administration;
- To increase use of partnerships between public, private, and voluntary sectors to implement regional policies.

This set of proposals reflects the profound changes in rural territories after World War II. Policymakers initially sought to foster the process of modernisation of rural areas, which were considered as a simple place of production (Guinjoan et al. 2016), but later began to focus on the competitiveness of rural areas within the concept of "economic growth" and the wider process of globalisation, particularly in Europe (Marsden 2006).

As noted by Wiskerke, food production, which has always been the main asset of rural territories, has undergone a transformation marked by three interconnected processes, namely (2009, pp. 370–371):

- *Disconnecting*, as distance and links between the producer and the consumer have increased.
- *Disembedding*, as the place of production has often lost its specificity and the local/regional character of foods is disappearing.
- *Disentwining*, as specialisation of supply chains has led to separated spheres of activities of goods and services.

Since the beginning of the twenty-first century, European policymakers have undertaken a different path, to promote "re-connection" (Winter 2003) and "re-territorialisation" (Horlings and Marsten 2012), processes that have given preference to place-based approaches; agriculture is increasingly seen in its role of maintaining "multifunctional green space and landscape quality" (Horlings and Marsten 2012, p. 2), while rural territories shift from "a homogeneous agricultural commodity market to a more segmented market" (Winter 2003, p. 506).

3.2 Characteristics of Rural Economies

Thus the concepts of "rural regions" (a spatial category) and "rural economies" do not necessarily, or almost never, refer to agriculture (a sector of economic activity): for example, as reported by Saraceno (1994), since the 1980s, there has been an increase in the number of non-farming jobs in defined rural areas of Italy (fewer than 3000 inhabitants as classified at that time). The commodification of rural areas is a quite recent phenomenon. The rapid urbanisation that took place between the 1950s and the 1990s in Europe (BBVA 2014) was followed by a counter-movement of people and capital towards peripheries in search of lower costs and better quality of life, a trend assisted by improved infrastructures and technologies, and by the globalisation process, which has reduced cultural differences. Consequently, the urban-rural dichotomy has been someway softened, particularly in relation to ideas of the modern and the traditional: Marini and Mooney define this new economy "as a 'patchwork' of diverse, local economies" (2006, p. 96), within which three ideal types of regional economies have arisen, namely

1. *Rent-seeking economies*, relying mostly on agriculture and extractive industries, therefore based on natural resources that do not require investments for diversified development. These economies are characterised by cultural resistance to change, sometimes geographical isolation, and low income. The shift to consumer-driven agriculture also penalises growth.
2. *Dependent economies*, which base their income on external resources. Dependence can be from either the public sector or private companies. Dependency causes a fragile economy: if the dependency is on the public sector, the economy suffers when the country's performance and ability to subsidise are compromised; if it is on private companies, which usually produce in the area because of the availability of cheap labour, it is vulnerable to investments or disinvestments in the area decided by a few.
3. *Entrepreneurial economies*, which produce wealth by valorising local traditional resources through modern or post-modern marketing structures (Brunori and Rossi 2000). In this type of economy, labour is not cheap and high standards of living often attract new residents from urban centres.

Rural development can then lead to various outcomes, and, even when external and internal pressures are intense, change never happens in mechanical ways. Social systems and local cultures react differently to strengths and opportunities provided by policies and regulatory regimes (Perkins 2006).

Regarding policies, the OECD (2018) identified the following "megatrends" likely to influence rural development in upcoming years:

- *Population ageing and migration*: the ageing phenomenon affects rural areas more than urban ones; besides, migration tends to flow towards urban centres more than to rural areas, and thus rural regions should seek to enhance their attractiveness to a new population;
- *Urbanisation*: although in past decades this process has stabilised, it could be further diminished by strengthening the links between urban and rural areas;
- *Global shifts in production*: rural regions need to invest in their specificities, increase the skills of their residents, and establish local-global links;

- *Rise of emerging economies*: emerging economies are expected to contribute to two-thirds of global growth by 2030. Their living standards will rise, and they will ask for new ways of sustainable production: rural areas will be asked to provide expertise to new markets. Also, more visitors and investors are expected to come to rural regions, which will need to strengthen relations with them;
- *Climate change and environmental pressures*: rural regions can take advantage of new technological shifts associated with green energy and circular economy;
- *Technological breakthroughs*: digital transformation will probably cause the loss of some kinds of jobs, but will foster demand for others in agriculture and services, such as the transportation of goods. Also, technology will open new ways of accessing services, diminishing the impact of geographical distance.

The OECD suggests that these mega-trends be addressed by policies to foster well-being in the economy, society, and the environment, seeking to downplay competition as an economic driver (as it was in the 2006's paradigm; see note 17). Also, previous policies favouring investments in qualified firms and communities will be replaced by an integrated rural development approach, which considers "(1) public sector—multi-level governance, (2) private sector—for-profit firms and social enterprise, and (3) the third sector—non-governmental organisations and civil society" (OECD 2018, p. 22). This new approach will most probably have a substantial impact on the shape of regional economies in the upcoming years.

3.3 Employment in Rural Economies

To better understanding how access to the labour market takes place via different pathways in various contexts, it is useful to introduce the concept of the local labour market. "Labour markets may be local or national (even international) in their scope and are made up of smaller, interacting labour markets for different qualifications, skills, and geographical locations. They depend on the exchange of information between employers and job seekers about wage rates, conditions of employment, level of competition, and job location" (Business dictionary).

Even if the gap between urban and rural is slowly narrowing, distinctive features of rural labour markets persist. According to Green (2016), and including findings from de Hoyos and Green (2011), specific factors characterise rural labour market both from the demand and supply side:

Demand-side:

- Weak service sector;
- Low availability of highly skilled workers compared to an over-supply of intermediary and low-skilled workers;
- Preponderance of SMEs and family businesses.

Supply-side:

- Ageing population, with new population composed more by retired persons who have migrated from the cities;
- Low resident qualified young workforce migrated elsewhere, looking for better work prospects and higher wages;
- Seasonal and "cheap" job offers, increasingly taken by migrants.

Furthermore, geographical and infrastructural features create difficulty in matching demand and supply, and most qualified young workers tend to leave to pursue better opportunities, because of:

- Limited transport and mobility (Hodge et al. 2002; Rugg and Jones 1999).
- Limited services, such as child and elder care, schools, and training opportunities (Green and Hardill 2003; Rugg and Jones 1999).
- Poor internet infrastructure (OECD 2014).

Rural areas are also marked by increasing numbers of self-employed residents. However, research has shown differences in self-employment and entrepreneurship in rural and urban areas. Faggio and Silva (2014) demonstrated that urban self-employment strongly correlates with business creation and innovation. Others suggest that rural areas are marked by "survival self-employment" (MacDonald 1996) motivated by lack of opportunities and alternatives, rather than by entrepreneurial drive (Green 2016; Tervo 2004; Hodge et al. 2002).

3.4 Job Seeking in Rural Settings

According to the literature, informal processes are the most effective way to access the labour market in rural areas: personal recommendations, word of mouth, and direct knowledge are the most common forms of recruitment (Hodge et al. 2002; Monk et al. 1999). Matthews et al. (2009, p. 326) compared paths to employment in urban and rural regions of Canada: they found that rural labour markets are "much more constrained and limited than those found in cities", and "strong and weak ties are used more frequently as paths to employment in rural regions". Additional candidate characteristics valued by employers are proximity (Monk et al. 1999), work experience gained on the job and not in formal education (Lindsay et al. 2003), and membership in a family that has been established in the area for a long time (Hodge et al. 2002).

However, Cartmel and Furlong (2000), on the basis of 40 interviews of employers carried out in four rural areas of the United Kingdom, argued that recruitment is also based on the professional profile needed and identified three broad categories:

- Recruiting for low-skilled jobs, which required low education and training levels, was performed mostly at the local level.
- Recruiting for semi-skilled jobs was performed at the local level in the pool of more educated or trained persons, who then were trained in-house.
- Recruiting for professional and managerial positions (a smaller number) was carried out on the national level, and hired staff had no connection with the local community.

Cartmel and Furlong (2000) also carried out 80 in-depth interviews with young people aged 15–24 in the same four UK rural areas. Their results confirmed the same barriers identified as values for employers (work experience, family reputation, and proximity to the job place) and the need to rely on social networks for finding information about jobs. They found that effective networking included both strong (family) and weak (friends, neighbours) ties. Other research confirms that the most effective channel for job hunting is networking (Matthews et al. 2009; Shucksmith 2004; Gerry et al. 2004; Lindsay et al. 2003), as it is essential for finding information about jobs. An additional barrier to work in rural areas is that wages are lower on average, and workers find that the costs of transportation and housing (Culliney 2017) can be unsustainable.

Yet another barrier to job seeking and employment, in general, is gender: women in rural areas still suffer from higher unemployment and lower wages of women compared to men and women living in urban areas (European Parliament 2019).

Graduates in rural areas are challenged by the mismatch between aspirations and the availability of high-skill jobs (Dax et al. 2002), and the phenomenon of out-migration is significant (Corbett 2007). However, some factors contribute to enabling the return of graduates to rural regions. Drawing on the works of Rérat (2014), Niedomysl and Amcoff (2011), and Looker and Naylor (2009), it can be argued that those "who return" to rural places after graduation do so for social reasons. Identity is constructed in place and through the experience of the lived world. So the space, as co-constitutive dimension (Farrugia 2014), and the strength of rural identity can figure significantly in the decisions of graduates to live where they grew up, to allow their children a life in this environment to which they belong. Also, ties with parents, relatives, and friends play a significant role in this respect. As Niedomysl and Amcoff (2011, p. 656) pointed out: "although there are indications that employment factors may facilitate return migration, return migration is largely driven by social considerations".

Notes

1. Densely populated: "contiguous set of local areas, each of which has a density superior to 500 inhabitants per square kilometre, where the total population for the set is at least 50,000 inhabitants"; Intermediate area: "contiguous set of local areas, not belonging to a densely-populated area, each of which has a density superior to 100 inhabitants per square kilometre, and either with a total population for the set of at least 50,000 inhabitants or adjacent to a densely-populated area"; Thinly populated: "set of local areas belonging neither to a densely-populated nor to an intermediate area" (Dijkstra and Poelman 2014, p. 17).
2. Local Administrative Units Level 2 are municipalities (Eurostat, 2017. See: https://ec.europa.eu/eurostat/web/nuts/local-administrative-units).
3. Grid cells that are not identified as urban centres or as urban clusters, where urban centres are "cluster of contiguous grid cells of 1 km^2 (excluding diagonals) with a population density of at least 1500 inhabitants per km^2 and collectively a minimum population of 50,000 inhabitants after gap-filling"

and urban clusters are "a cluster of contiguous grid cells of 1 km^2 (including diagonals) with a population density of at least 300 inhabitants per km^2 and a minimum population of 5000 inhabitants" (Eurostat Glossary, retrieved online October 2019).

4. https://ec.europa.eu/agriculture/rural-development-2014-2020_en.
5. The previous framework proposed by OECD was the "New rural development paradigm" (2006), and it was characterised by a policy planning based on competitiveness.

References

Alexander Wandl, D. I., Nadin, V., Zonneveld, W., & Rooij, R. (2014). Beyond Urban–Rural Classifications: Characterising and Mapping Territories-in-Between Across Europe. *Landscape and Urban Planning, 130*, 50–63.

BBVA. (2014). *Urbanization Report. European Urbanization Trends*. Madrid: BBVA Research.

Brunori, G., & Rossi, A. (2000). Synergy and Coherence Through Collective Action: Some Insights from Wine Routes in Tuscany. *Sociologia Ruralis, 40*(4), 409–423.

Cartmel, F., & Furlong, A. (2000). *Youth Unemployment in Rural Areas*. Work and Opportunity Series No. 18. York: Joseph Rowntree Foundation.

Corbett, M. (2007). All Kinds of Potential: Women and Out-Migration in an Atlantic Canadian Coastal Community. *Journal of Rural Studies, 23*(4), 430–442.

Culliney, M. (2017). Escaping the Rural Pay Penalty: Location, Migration and the Labour Market. *Work, Employment and Society, 31*(3), 429–446.

Dax, T., Machold, I., & Gerry, C. (2002). 'Youth Spirit'—The Ingredient That Makes All the Difference? In T. Dax & I. Machold (Eds.), *Voices of Rural Youth: A Break with Traditional Patterns?* Wien: Bundesanstalt für Bergbauernfragen.

de Hoyos, M., & Green, A. (2011). Recruitment and Retention Issues in Rural Labour Markets. *Journal of Rural Studies, 27*(2), 171–180.

Dijkstra, L., & Poelman, H. (2014). *A Harmonised Definition of Cities and Rural Areas: The New Degree of Urbanisation*. Regional Working Paper 2014, WP 01/2014, European Commission.

European Parliament. (2019). *The Professional Status of Rural Women in the EU*. Policy Department for Citizens' Rights and Constitutional Affairs, Directorate General for Internal Policies of the Union, PE 608.868.

Eurostat (2017). Statistics on Rural Areas in the EU. *Eurostat Statistics Explained*. https://ec.europa.eu/eurostat/statistics-explained/index.php/Statistics_on_rural_areas_in_the_EU

Faggio, G., & Silva, O. (2014). Self-Employment and Entrepreneurship in Urban and Rural Labour Markets. *Journal of Urban Economics, 84*, 67–85.

Farrugia, D. (2014). Towards a Spatialised Youth Sociology: The Rural and the Urban in Times of Change. *Journal of Youth Studies, 17*(3), 293–307.

Garrett, J. (2005). *Beyond rural urban. Keeping up with changing realities.* Washington: International Food Policy Research Institute.

Gerry, C., Antonio, P., Marques, C., Portela, J., & Rebelo, V. (2004). Social Networks, Labour Market and Policy Impact in Santa Marta de Peneguaio. In B. Jentsch & M. Shucksmith (Eds.), *Young People in Rural Areas of Europe, Ashgate Perspectives on Rural Policy and Planning*. Aldershot Hants: Ashgate Publishing Limited.

Green, A. (2016). Changing Dynamics of Rural Labour Markets. In M. Shucksmith & D. L. Brown (Eds.), *Routledge International Handbook of Rural Studies.* London: Routledge.

Green, A. E., & Hardill, I. (2003). *Rural Labour Markets, Skills and Training.* Coventry: Warwick Institute for Employment Research.

Guinjoan, E., Badia, A., & Tulla, A. (2016). The New Paradigm of Rural Development. *Theoretical Considerations and Reconceptualization Using the 'Rural Web', 71*, 495–500.

Hodge, I., Dunn, J., Monk, S., & Fitzgerald, M. (2002). Barriers to Participation in Residual Labour Markets. *Work, Employment and Society, 16*, 457–476.

Horlings, J., & Marsten, T. (2012). Exploring the 'New Rural Paradigm' in Europe: Eco-Economic Strategies as a Counterforce to the Global Competitiveness Agenda. *European Urban and Regional Studies, 0*(0), 1–17.

Lindsay, C., McCracken, M., & McQuaid, R. W. (2003). Unemployment Duration and Employability in Remote Rural Labour Markets. *Journal of Rural Studies, 19*, 187–200.

Looker, D., & Naylor, T. (2009). 'At Risk' of Being Rural? The Experience of Rural Youth in a Risk Society. *Journal of Rural and Community Development, 4*(2), 39–64.

MacDonald, R. (1996). Welfare Dependency, the Enterprise Culture and Self-Employed Survival. *Work, Employment and Society, 10*(3), 431–447.

Marini, B. M., & Mooney, P. H. (2006). Rural Economies. In P. Cloke, T. Marsden, & P. Mooney (Eds.), *The Handbook of Rural Studies.* London: SAGE Publications.

Marsden, T. (2006). Denial or Diversity? Creating New Spaces for Sustainable Development. *Journal of Environmental Policy & Planning, 8*(2), 183–198.

Matthews, R., Pendakur, R., & Young, N. (2009). Social Capital, Labour Markets, and Job-Finding in Urban and Rural Regions: Comparing Paths to Employment in Prosperous Cities and Stressed Rural Communities in Canada. *The Sociological Review, 57*, 2.

Monk, S., Dunn, J., Fizgerald, M., & Hodge, I. (1999). *Finding Work in Rural Areas: Barriers and Bridges.* Work and Opportunity Series No. 13. York: York Publishing Services for the Joseph Rowntree Foundation.

Niedomysl, T., & Amcoff, J. (2011). Why Return Migrants Return: Survey Evidence on Motives for Internal Return Migration in Sweden. *Population, Space and Place, 17*, 656–673.

OECD. (2014). *Innovation and Modernising the Rural Economy.* Paris: OECD.

OECD. (2018). *Rural 3.0. A Framework for Rural Development.* Policy Note. Retrieved October 4, 2019, from https://www.oecd.org/cfe/regional-policy/Rural-3.0-Policy-Note.pdf.

Perkins, H. (2006). Commodification: Re-Resourcing Rural Areas. In P. In Cloke, T. Marsden, & P. Mooney (Eds.), *The Handbook of Rural Studies.* London: SAGE Publications.

Rérat, P. (2014). The Selective Migration of Young Graduates: Which of Them Return to Their Rural Home Region and Which do Not? *Journal of Rural Studies, 35*, 123–132.

Rugg, J., & Jones, A. (1999). *Getting a Job, Finding a Home: Rural Youth Transitions.* York: Joseph Tree Foundation.

Saraceno, E. (1994). The Modern Functions of Small Farm Systems: An Italian Experience. *Sociologia Ruralis, 34*, 4.

Shucksmith, M. (2004). Young People and Social Exclusion in Rural Areas. *Sociologia Ruralis, 44*, 1.

Tervo, H. (2004). *Self-Employment Dynamics in Rural and Urban Labour Markets.* ERSA Conference Papers from European Regional Science Association. Retrieved from http://www-sre.wu.ac.at/ersa/ersaconfs/ersa04/PDF/396.pdf.

Whitaker, W. H. (1982). *The Many Faces of Ephraim: In Search of a Functional Typology of Rural Areas.* (ERIC Document Reproduction Service No. ED242459).

Winter, M. (2003). Geographies of Food: Agro-Food Geographies—Making Reconnections. *Progress in Human Geography, 27*(4), 505–513.

Wiskerke, J. S. C. (2009). On Places Lost and Places Regained: Reflections on the Alternative Food Geography and Sustainable Regional Development. *International Planning Studies, 14*, 369–387.

CHAPTER 4

Higher Education and Employability

Abstract In response to many demands about their role within society, in the past few decades universities have reviewed and changed curricula and teaching methods, and created, improved, or diversified initiatives to link with reference territories. In this ongoing effort, universities need to address the issue of their own "new role" and identity within a continuously changing society. This chapter outlines the key themes of the "changing university" by focusing on the employability issue, looking at emerging employability models, and reporting on the current debate about the role of the university within the social system.

Keywords Employability models • Career centres • Accountability • Mission

4.1 Higher Education and Employability

4.1.1 *"The Change" in Practice*

Higher-education institutions have reacted to new demands in different ways, according to their systems, geographical location, and capacity to embrace input.

Universities are per se providers of forms of knowledge, credentials (they are legitimised to issue degrees), and supplementary learning (e.g. through career services) (Tomlinson 2013). Concerning forms of

G. Paviotti, *'Regional Universities' and Pedagogy*,
https://doi.org/10.1007/978-3-030-53680-0_4

knowledge, the university provides curricula to transmit, transform, and create new knowledge in a specific field. Universities also have freedom in proposing "legitimate" degrees: the university degree is a credential. Curricula can include direct relations with the labour market, by formulating degrees answering new learning needs (e.g. Chyung et al. 2006), or can focus on the liberal arts, which are not directly linked with specific professions (e.g. Fallows and Stevens 2000). In some cases, though, new curricula are developed more to attract students than to respond to research-based knowledge or labour market requests (Rae 2007). Also, alongside hard skills provided through curricula, universities support the development of transversal skills, usually through active pedagogies and work-based learning. Finally, supplementary learning opportunities are offered, through university centres or other extra-curricular activities. Students, though, can perceive these opportunities as "unconnected" to the degree (Rae 2007).

All these dimensions have been considered by several studies that provided different frameworks for higher-education institutions for employability purposes. In 2003, Yorke proposed the following ways to assess employability integration in the curriculum, acknowledging that the distinctions among them are not clear-cut:

- Employability through the whole curriculum.[1]
- Employability in the core curriculum, for example, by applying the USEM model (see below), embedding employability in core modules of the curriculum.
- Work-based or work-related learning, such as internships.
- Employability-related modules within the curriculum.
- Work-based or work-related learning in parallel with the curriculum, for example, part-time jobs.

Yorke's work was carried out in the frame of the policy action of the United Kingdom towards employability. The Higher Education Academy Framework focuses on "embedding employability as providing the opportunities to develop knowledge, skills, experiences, behaviours, attributes, achievements and attitudes to enable graduates to make successful transitions and contributions, benefitting them, the economy and their communities".[2] The Higher Education Academy provides tools and resources for undertaking the programme to integrate the framework into institutions, consultancy in case of request, and a meeting point for a community of practice.

The proposed framework is based on three overarching principles—inclusivity, collaboration and engagement—and implemented in four stages:

1. Defining employability: this stage was aimed at creating shared knowledge within the institution (or department, or another level of action) and its stakeholders, to develop a working model for employability and assign activities and responsibilities.
2. Auditing and mapping: in this stage review and mapping of the resources needed to apply the model are carried out. It includes courses, students' perceptions, internal sharing, revision of curricula, and so on, and identifies gaps between the working model and the actual situation.
3. Prioritising actions: this is the stage for planning the activities needed to achieve the goals defined in step one and includes staff, students, and stakeholders.
4. Measuring impact: the final stage refers to mechanisms for monitoring and evaluation to assess progress and achievements.

The process of implementation, although linear in its development, is hindered by several factors in the structure and culture of higher-education institutions. In fact, according to Rae (2007), universities are still "disaggregated systems" in which educational offer, support services, and departments are not always connected. Employability is the result of a "holistic learning experience" (2007, p. 608) that is not limited to a specific program of study. Activities not directly connected to curricular courses, particularly those provided by career centres, may be perceived by students as unconnected, also considering that they are managed by different people "who in a large university may rarely meet" (2007, p. 608).

It is worth recalling that while the United Kingdom has carried out specific actions for employability in higher education, other countries could have less guidance on the topic. Many considerations about universities can be shared across all European higher-education institutions, but national situations differently shape the employability issue. An example of this difference is Italy. In Italy, neoliberal policies in higher education started in the 1990s, however with a slow pace. According to Scacchi et al. (2017), the process began with autonomy and market orientation, by decreeing competitive autonomy between institutions (1990–1995); a second step was the reform of teaching organisation and included internal evaluation and the establishment of quality processes (1996–2005); a third step addressed the reform of the academic staff recruitment and the reduction of funding (2006–present). For several reasons, depending on the culture and on the fact that educational policies are most focused on school than on tertiary education, the country is still in a "transitional period" (Scacchi et al. 2017, p. 211). This overall framework also explains the fact that specific employability policies have never been implemented. Employability is present in the general debate about university, and more popular in the media discourse than at policy level. The national evaluation system (the basis for higher-education system funding) has included only recently (2019–2020) items on employability of graduates, even if data were collected since several years. This approach also results in a different meaning and value of employability in higher education in the perceptions of universities. The students are also part of these perceptions: first, the Italian student is never considered "a client", as in some other countries, but as a learner; second, if the university is still an investment, it does not require high stakes for the fees, although it is not completely free. All this results in a real different perception of employability term, which is more used in the employment field than in the education field.

Europe has many differences across educational systems, the way they are implemented, the way they are perceived. Some processes, such as the push towards "change" (e.g. regional dimension, curricula linked with the labour market), are common, but actual "changes" are very place-based.

4.1.2 Employability Models

Researchers have also put considerable effort into trying to develop reliable approaches, or models, to support the acquisition of skills for employability. The most known and used in higher education are the following:

The DOTS Model
Developed by Law and Watts (1977), it is based on career development principles that should be applied in higher education. It includes:

- **D**ecision-making (being able to weigh up personal factors to make a sound plan).
- **O**pportunity awareness (knowledge of opportunities and the ability to research these).

- **T**ransition learning (understanding of how to seek and secure opportunities).
- **S**elf-awareness (the ability to identify and articulate motivations, skills, and personality as they affect career plans).

The four areas are mostly a reference for career and support services in higher education (e.g. QAA 2001), but some attempt has also been made to integrate them into the curriculum (Rae 2007) or to use them for policy analysis (Hillage and Pollard 1998).

The USEM Model
USEM (Yorke & Knight 2004, Knight & Yorke 2002) is an acronym for the following employability components:

- **U**nderstanding
- **S**kills (subject-specific and generic)
- **E**fficacy (beliefs and self-theories generally)
- **M**etacognition (including reflection)

Understanding, skills, and metacognition are mutually supportive and developmental. The efficacy component encompasses personal qualities such as the ability to face and solve a problem, or the willingness to learn, which are assets that "pervade employability" in any situation (2002, p. 226).

The adoption of the USEM model implies a switch in the way of teaching, more than in what is taught. The authors also stress the need to make explicit the link between the activities and employability skills development.

The Career Edge Model
Dacre Pool and Sewell (2007) developed this model, composed by the words "**Career** Development Learning" and the acronym EDGE:

- **E**xperience (Work & Life)
- **D**egree Subject Knowledge, Understanding & Skills
- **G**eneric Skills
- **E**motional Intelligence

Those components should be completed with "reflection and evaluation" activities to enhance:

- Self-reflection
- Self-confidence
- Self-esteem

The most significant novelty of this model is the insertion of "emotional intelligence", which in the USEM model is included in "personal qualities", defined, according to Mayer et al. (2004, p. 167), as "the capacity to reason about emotions, and of emotions to enhance thinking. It includes the abilities to accurately perceive emotions, to access and generate emotions to assist thought, to understand emotions and emotional knowledge, and to reflectively regulate emotions to promote emotional and intellectual growth".

These models, however, appear to be reference frameworks with little advice on how to implement activities leading to the employability objectives. In particular, for areas such as "personal qualities", or "generic skills" it is hard to apply focused learning provisions, as there is little scientific evidence on how to assess them effectively.

Additionally, evaluating the impact of employability strategies within institutions is a difficult task. In 2016, the Warwick Institute of Employment Research (UK) undertook a study to assess the efficacy of employability provisions by consulting employers (31), education providers (83 universities, 52 FE colleges providing HE and 17 alternative providers), and students (51), and analysing their input. The study examined the following aspects offered by education providers:

- Information services (announcements of job vacancies).
- Assistance with CVs, application form completion, and so on.
- Skill development (e.g. support for developing presentation skills).
- Work experience (e.g. internships/placements).
- Recording achievement (in the United Kingdom the Higher Education Achievement Report, which is a portfolio).
- Services aimed specifically at postgraduates.

The researchers found that there was high or very high provision of these services. However, employers stressed that graduate competencies do not match their needs, and noted a lack of presentation skills, for example, mistakes and inaccuracies in applications. Students are resistant to engagement—those who already have career plans believe that career services are not relevant to them. In contrast, those whose intentions are yet undefined prefer to focus on their academic work. The authors of the study noted that "an assessment is difficult to undertake given the lack of data that links employability provision to student employment outcomes". Also, employment outcomes would not be enough: the relative dimension composed by the economy of the places also plays a role on the figure.

4.2 The Role of Career and Support Services

As noted above, offices providing career-related services have a clear purpose in employability provisions within the higher-education system.

According to Dey and Cruzvergara (2014), career services evolved in six phases from 1900 to date (2014, pp. 2–8):

- 1900–1920 Vocational Guidance
- 1920–1940 Teachers Guidance
- 1940–1970 Job Placement
- 1970–1990 Career Counselling
- 1990–2010 Professional Networking
- 2010–... Connected Communities

During the first two periods, there was no such thing as a career centre: non-university entities provided vocational guidance, and university faculties assisted graduating teachers.[3] In the next period, career services became part of the universities' offer (Kretovicks et al. 1999). The boom of the post-war economy required a larger workforce, and job placement became the first mission of career services. From the 1940s to about 1970, the in loco parentis approach to placement was the most dominant, while in the 1970s and 1980s the developmental model came to the fore, changing the focus from parenting students to developing them (Kretovicks et al. 1999, p. 80). Career counselling was the approach of these decades, but placement was more a consequence than an objective of student development. After 1990, as the role of the university changed, so did that of career centres, and they consequently modified their approaches and activities to foster links with employers, organising networking events, job fairs, and other recruiting activities (Dey and Real 2009). In response to the recession that began in 2008, career services increased their work to support the development of a civic, engaged, and entrepreneurial university (Dey and Cruzvergara 2014), promoting new connections with different sectors as well as networks and partnerships among enterprises, students, and alumni.

All along, of course, career centres have continued to offer career counselling, workshops, and assistance for curriculum writing, and also career fairs and placement opportunities. Career centres support students and new graduates in developing skills precisely related to career development and job-seeking, and in most cases are directly in charge of placements.

Research has not yet explored in-depth the relations between career services and pedagogies. A recent project funded by the Ministry of Education in Italy (PRIN EMP&CO—Employability and Competences[4]) looked at a more comprehensive view of the university's "employability offer". The conclusion was that employability is achieved through a process that encompasses the higher-education experience as a whole. All forms of learning—be they through formal, non-formal, or informal settings, in the classroom or through internships and placements—contribute to the same goal (Boffo 2018, pp. 124–125). Career advice and support are also a significant part of the overall process (Federighi 2018, p. 142).

4.3 "What Are Universities For?"

The title makes explicit reference to the Collini's book published in 2012. The question is still valid and open to debate: until the nineteenth century, the function of the university was to create knowledge (as in Newman 1852, cited by McCowan 2015, p. 10). Then, alongside the knowledge production (intrinsic value), the universities started to have more instrumental functions (instrumental value) for the benefit of society (Dunne 2006; Collini 2012; McCowan 2015). The two values are not opposed: also academic research has always been driven by social needs and responsive to society, perhaps in a way less clearly stated (or wished) than today (William-Jones 2005; Nedeva 2007; Collini 2012). The critical point is the balance of these values. Regarding academic research, Nedeva (2007) wondered if research conducted with private funds, or in technological clusters, serves the public good or the private one. Regarding employability, Morley (2001) warned of the risk of a university aimed at producing workers more than at educating citizens. Also, the idea that an individual is "ready for work" just after graduation, as expected by employers, is questioned, as many skills can be acquirable only on the job (Mason et al.

2009; Tymon 2013). Also, some authors argued that the university provides general skills and attitudes which are valuable on the job (Ng and Feldman 2009), whereby how much education can directly increase the job performance, in terms of productivity, remains unclear.

The need for the university to give evidence of its "usefulness" in both research and teaching (Kreber 2006) led to the idea that research should result as an automatic product development and teaching should have as outcome employment (concerning public investment) and higher income (regarding students views). This mechanism is not perhaps stated as such by policies, but it is implicit in some approaches and resolutions, and it is generally the approach of business. The tension between educational and business systems is still high, and it seems that the dialogue, which was supposed to increase following third mission and regionalisation of universities, have had little progress over the years on this issue. Jackson noted that the point is not much which competences can be (or not) developed in higher education, but how much "the work environment enables the graduate to 'unleash' these developed competencies" (2009, p. 4). The commitment over employability should be from both sides, and find resistances from both sides as well.

Given the pressing demands on higher education, and the reduction of funding that has redesigned much of the university strategies, this resistance is not surprising. It involves the very nature of the university and requires a constructive debate within the university community: the primary mission of teaching in higher education is to educate citizen. However, career education allows citizens to contribute to society also through work. Highly educated citizens can remarkably contribute to a sustainable world through their expression and way of acting in daily life. Relations with business should be re-framed, and both sides need to redefine roles and identities looking at common goals of development.

Notes

1. The reference model here is the Alverno College in the United States, which requires students to develop eight broad "abilities" through the curriculum, namely communication, problem solving, social interaction, effective citizenship, analysis, valuing, developing a global perspective, and aesthetic engagement (https://www.alverno.edu/academics/ouruniquecurriculum/the8coreabilities/).

2. Website of the HEA: https://www.heacademy.ac.uk/individuals/strategic-priorities/employability.
3. In 1908 the Civic Service House of Boston opened the unit Vocation Bureau, which was aimed at providing educational guidance to train them for work. The Vocation Bureau is acknowledged as the first "career centre" in history (Kretovicks et al. 1999; Wilson 2013).
4. https://empecoprin.it/.

References

Boffo, V. (2018). Employability and Transitions: Fostering the Future of Young Adult Graduates. In V. Boffo & M. Fedeli (Eds.), *Employability & Competences. Innovative Curricula for New Professions* (pp. 117–128). Firenze: Firenze University Press.

Chyung, S. Y., Stepich, D., & Cox, D. (2006). Building a Competency-Based Curriculum Architecture to Educate 21st-Century Business Practitioners. *Journal of Education for Business, 81*(6), 307–314.

Collini, S. (2012). *What Are Universities For?* London: Penguin.

Dacre Pool, L., & Sewell, P. J. (2007). The Key to Employability: Developing a Practical Model of Graduate Employability. *Education + Training, 49*(4), 277–289.

Dey, F., & Cruzvergara, C. Y. (2014). *Evolution of Career Services in Higher Education*. New Directions for Student Services, 148, Winter 2014, Wiley Periodicals, Inc.

Dey, F., & Real, M. (2009). *Adaptation of Casella's Model: Emerging Trends in Career Services*. Presentation online Retrieved from http://www.myacpa.org/sites/default/files/Casella%20Adaptation%20Presentation.pdf.

Dunne, J. (2006). Newman Now: Re-Examining the Concepts of 'Philosophical' and 'Liberal' in the Idea of a University. *British Journal of Educational Studies, 54*(4), 412–428.

Fallows, S., & Steven, C. (2000). Building Employability Skills Into the Higher Education Curriculum: A University-Wide Initiative. *Education + Training, 42*(2), 75–83.

Federighi, P. (2018). Non-linear Paths in Transitions through the Labour Market. In V. Boffo & M. Fedeli (Eds.), *Employability & Competences. Innovative Curricula for New Professions* (pp. 129–147). Firenze: Firenze University Press.

Hillage, J., & Pollard, E. (1998). *Employability: Developing a Framework for Policy Analysis*. Research Report RR85. London: Department for Education and Employment.

Jackson, D. (2009). Profiling Industry-Relevant Management Graduate Competencies: The Need for a Fresh Approach. *International Journal of Management Education, 8*(1), 85–98.

Knight, P. T., & Yorke, M. (2002). Employability Through the Curriculum. *Tertiary Education and Management, 8*, 261–276, Netherlands: Kluwer Academic Publishers.

Kreber, C. (2006). Setting the Context: The Climate of University Teaching and Learning. *New Directions for Higher Education, 133*, 5–11.

Kretovicks, M., Honaker, S., & Kraning, J. (1999). Career Centers: Changing Needs Require Changing Paradigms. *Journal of Student Affairs at Colorado State University, 8*, 77–84.

Law, B., & Watts, A. G. (1977). *Schools, Careers and Community*. London: Church Information Office.

Mason, G., Williams, G., & Cranmer, S. (2009). Employability Skills Initiatives in Higher Education: What Effects Do They Have on Graduate Labour Market Outcomes? *Education Economics, 17*(1), 1–30.

Mayer, J. D., Salovey, P., & Caruso, D. R. (2004). Emotional Intelligence: Theory, Findings, and Implications. *Psychological Inquiry, 15*(3), 197–215.

McCowan, T. (2015). Should Universities Promote Employability? *Theory and Research in Education, 13*(3), 267–285.

Morley, L. (2001). Producing New Workers: Quality, Equality and Employability in Higher Education. *Quality in Higher Education, 7*(2), 131–138.

Nedeva, M. (2007). New Tricks and Old Dogs: The 'Third Mission' and the Reproduction of the University. In D. Epstein, R. Boden, R. Deem, F. Rizvi, & S. Wright (Eds.), *The World Yearbook of Education 2008: Geographies of Knowledge/Geometries of Power—Higher Education in the 21st Century* (pp. 85–104). New York: Routledge.

Newman, J. H. (1852). *The Idea of the University Defined and Illustrated In Nine Discourses Delivered to the Catholics of Dublin*, London: Longmans, Green and Co.

Ng, T. W. H., & Feldman, D. (2009). How Broadly Does Education Contribute to Job Performance? *Personnel Psychology, 62*, 89–134.

Quality Assurance Agency—QAA. (2001). *Code of Practice Section 8, Careers Education, Information and Guidance.*

Rae, D. (2007). Connecting Enterprise and Graduate Employability: Challenges to the Higher Education Culture and Curriculum? *Education + Training, 49*(8/9), 605–619.

Scacchi, L., Benozzo, A., Carbone, D., & Monaci, M. G. (2017). Neo-Liberalism in the Italian University: Encroachment and Resistance. *Cultural Studies Critical Methodologies, 17*(3), 205–213.

Tomlinson, M. (2013). *Education, Work and Identity*. London: Bloomsbury.

Tymon, A. (2013). The Student Perspective on Employability. *Studies in Higher Education, 38*(6), 841–856.

William-Jones, B. (2005). Knowledge Commons or Economic Engine—What's a University For? *Journal of Medical Ethics, 31*(5), 249–250.

Wilson, F. (2013). *The Creation of the National Vocational Guidance Association*. Article Posted on the Website of National Career Development Association. Retrieved from https://www.ncda.org/aws/NCDA/pt/sd/news_article/74076/_PARENT/CC_layout_details/false.

Yorke, M., & Knight, P. T. (2004). *Embedding Employability into the Curriculum*. York: The Higher Education Academy.

CHAPTER 5

The Employers

Abstract This chapter addresses the second principal component of the meso-level of graduate employability, the business world. Recent changes in the labour market from a business perspective are described. Companies, challenged by the global economy and the increased competition, also underwent structural changes. "Flexibility" has become a crucial concept. New ways of working and employment relations have changed recruitment systems. Also the size of enterprises, which impacts both recruitment and attraction of graduates, is explored. Some considerations on skills mismatch are finally introduced.

Keywords Employers • Flexibility • Recruitment • SMEs • Skills mismatch

5.1 The Changing Labour Market: Employers' Perspective

As outlined in Chap. 1, the labour market has experienced a dramatic change in past decades: high competition, global challenges, and increased automation affect companies, who ask for a flexible and mobile workforce, and consequent deregulation of labour contracts.

Flexibility, according to the best-known model (Atkinson 1984, p. 3), can be seen from three points of view:

G. Paviotti, *'Regional Universities' and Pedagogy*,
https://doi.org/10.1007/978-3-030-53680-0_5

1. Functional flexibility, such that the employees "can be redeployed quickly and smoothly between activities and tasks".
2. Numerical flexibility, allowing hiring and firing to be quick and easy.
3. Financial flexibility, which has two aspects: the first is related to possible variations in employment costs concerning the external market; the second is associated with the pay system for new forms of pay calculations, for example, assessment-based.

To achieve **functional flexibility**, businesses seek employees who possess a more comprehensive range of competences to fulfil not only their job, but, if needed, that of others. It means changing rapidly to adapt to shifts in the labour market (Valverde et al. 2000), and thus requires workers to be more responsible and autonomous, to possess the ability to learn to learn, and to engage in lifelong learning to stay competitive.

As regards **numerical flexibility**, in the 1980s, several European countries attempted to deregulate labour markets, as "law, regulation and institutions were considered barriers to sound economic development and growth" (Wilthangen and Tros 2004, p. 7).[1] Deregulation of the labour market, however, has meant less social protection in most cases, weakening the European social model.[2] To this end, the European Union has worked towards policies to improve *flexibility* provisions across countries (Philips and Eamets 2007; Tangian 2008). "Flexicurity" can be defined as "a policy strategy that attempts, synchronically and in a deliberate way, to enhance the flexibility of the labour market and to enhance security—employment security and social security—notably for weaker groups inside and outside the labour market" (Wilthangen and Tros 2004, p. 5). The concept includes more than just labour agreements or contracts: it implies a system able to align welfare provisions such as unemployment benefits, active labour policies to support job insertion and lifelong learning opportunities, and sound industrial relations with enterprises. *Flexicurity* provisions have good outcomes in Scandinavian countries and those with liberal traditions like the Netherlands. In other countries, particularly the Mediterranean group, deregulation of the labour market has not been embedded in a system-wide provision, or at least not to a sufficient extent (see Philips and Eamets 2007, pp. 29–30 for countries groups related to *flexicurity*). The outcome has been the emergence of a dual labour market.[3]

Finally, regarding **financial flexibility**, the most common efforts to achieve it have tied worker benefits to the performance of the firm, a method also accepted by trade unions. Instead, variable pay is less applied, first, because it requires performance appraisal systems which would be hard to design and implement, and second, because of the resistance of trade unions and worker representatives, who see in those schemes a risk for the minimum wage (Valverde et al. 2000).

5.2 The Employers' Expectations on Graduates

Understanding the expectations of employers to better design curricula and prepare graduates for smooth transitions to work has been subject to many studies. Some of these studies have been carried out at the national level and promoted by governments or other public bodies, for example, the National Skills Survey in the United Kingdom,[4] and others at business level, assisted by international or national agencies and associations, such as the World Economic Forum[5] or the Excelsior system[6] in Italy, which, however, focus more on the workforce than on skills.

Surveys and analyses can be roughly divided into two areas:

- Sector-based, which look at specific skills required for a working area.
- Skills-based, which look at the market overall, and often are related to soft and other transversal skills.

Both perspectives try to anticipate labour market needs in the future, to avoid as much as possible skills mismatches and skills shortages. Besides, data obtained in these studies are expected to provide a better understanding of how to increase the employability of graduates through the curriculum.

Sector-based surveys are common in technical and scientific degrees, such as engineering and construction (e.g. Kranov and Khalaf 2016; Davies et al. 1999), IT (e.g. Hamilton et al. 2015), and science, including bioscience and biotechnology (e.g. Saunders and Zuzel 2010). As regards the liberal arts, data are included in general surveys on graduates, since there is no direct link with specific professions.

Many skills-based surveys have relied on large numbers of respondents:

- The Gallup Organisation (2010)[7] surveyed 7036 companies in Europe-28, as well as Turkey, Norway, and Iceland, upon the request of the Directorate-General for Education and Culture (European Commission). Of the companies, 76% were medium-sized (50–249 employees), and the rest were large (250 or more employees), with the largest share active in industry (36%), non-public services (23%), and public services (17%). Findings highlighted the following key results (selected from a broader range of topics): the skill considered relevant by the highest percentage of respondents was "teamworking (67%), while 58% to 62% of respondents indicated sector-specific skills, communication skills, computer literacy, being able to adapt to new situations, first-class ability in reading/writing, and analytical and problem-solving skills". A lower percentage indicated skills in foreign languages to be significant (33–36% rated them very important or important). Fully 87% of the sample rated work experience as important. Regarding university involvement, only 6–8% of respondents indicated that they interacted with higher-education institutions frequently or rather frequently, an indication that curriculum design puts little emphasis on university cooperation with businesses. Instead, 52% of respondents viewed recruitment participation in internship programmes to be one of the best ways of cooperating with higher-education institutions.

- Archer and Davison (2008) surveyed 233 employers, of whom 43% were small companies with fewer than 100 employees, 27% were medium companies with 101–1000 employees, and 30% were large companies with over 1000 employees. The study summary concludes that: "86% of employers consider good communication skills to be important, yet many employers expressed dissatisfaction because graduates cannot express themselves effectively". "Soft" skills, such as team working, are also vital and even more important than most "hard" skills, although numeracy and literacy skills were considered essential by 70% of employers. Sixty-five percent of international employers indicate that having overseas professional work experience makes graduates more employable. Online recruitment is the most frequently used and most effective method of graduate recruitment (2008, p. 6).

These two surveys are examples of a larger number carried out in Europe (CEDEFOP 2013) or some OECD countries (Mourshed et al. 2012), or at a national level (the Employers Skills Survey in the United Kingdom[8]). In general, it could be said that employers tend to value transversal skills, and above all soft skills, as well as the various kinds of literacy skills (literacy, numeracy, scientific literacy, ICT literacy, financial literacy, cultural and civic literacy). This general, although not specific, agreement on skills needed for the labour market is evident in Table 5.1, highlighting similarities among the results of three major surveys:

It should be noted that there are reliable tools for assessing hard skills and literacy skills, but this is not the case for soft and personal skills.

Table 5.1 Comparison of survey results for the most important skills for work

World Economic Forum (skills for the twenty-first century)	*National Association of Colleges and Employers (NACE)*	*Employers' skills survey (2017)—list by detected skills needs*
Literacy Numeracy Scientific literacy ICT literacy Financial literacy Cultural and civic literacy Critical thinking/ problem solving Creativity Communication Collaboration Curiosity Initiative Persistence/grit Adaptability Leadership Social and cultural awareness	Ability to work in a team structure Ability to make decisions and solve problems Ability to plan, organize, and prioritize work Ability to obtain and process information Ability to analyse quantitative data Technical knowledge related to the job Proficiency with computer software programs Ability to create and/ or edit written reports	Specialist skills or knowledge needed to perform the role Ability to manage own time and prioritise own tasks Customer handling skills Solving complex problems requiring a solution specific to the situation Knowledge of products and services offered by your organisation and organisations like yours Team working Managing their own feelings, or handling the feelings of others Managing or motivating other staff Knowledge of how your organisation works Persuading or influencing others Reading and understanding instructions, guidelines, manuals, or reports Sales skills Writing instructions, guidelines, manuals, or reports Basic numerical skills and understanding More complex numerical or statistical skills and understanding Setting objectives for others and planning human, financial, and other resources Instructing, teaching, or training people Adapting to new equipment or materials Computer literacy/basic IT skills Advanced or specialist IT skills Manual dexterity Making speeches or presentations Communicating in a foreign language

5.3 Recruitment Strategies and the Concept of Work Readiness

Having identified many of the needs of employers, we turn to an examination of how employers make recruiting and selection decisions, and in particular, how companies attract graduates and why a graduate is selected among others.

In general, human capital theory (Schultz 1971; Becker 1994) or job market signalling theory (Spence 1973) regarding credentials (educational attainment) and work is applied.

The human capital theory is based on the idea that education increases job performance; therefore, individuals with higher educational attainments are more successful in the labour market, with more opportunities and higher income. Thus, from the point of view of the individual, education is an investment for a better position in the market, while for employers, it provides a tool for quantifying credentials. However, as pointed out by Levhari and Weiss (1974), employers often do not automatically recognise credentials as the key asset for the job. Employers consider that they are hiring human resources in a state of uncertainty, with uncertain inputs such as individual characteristics or quality of schooling, and unpredictable outputs such as future demand and supply conditions.

The job market signalling theory focuses instead on the relation between the graduate and the employer, for whom hiring a new employee always implies a certain level of risk. Spence distinguishes between indices, which the job candidate cannot change, and signals, which are mutable:

> [I shall refer to] observable, unalterable attributes as indices, reserving the term signals for those observable characteristics attached to the individual that are subject to manipulation by him. Some attributes, like age, do change, but not at the discretion of the individual. In my terms, these are indices. (1973, p. 357)

Credentials are signals: in presenting credentials, applicants reveal a part of the information about themselves that implicitly claims strong ability as workers. The employer, on the basis of previous hiring experience and the employee characteristics, interprets the signal(s) through what Spence calls "conditional probabilistic beliefs with respect to productivity".

Beliefs are also central to the model of Bailly (2008), who, starting from Spence's considerations, argues that employers' "beliefs and representations, particularly about the origin of the qualities individuals require in the workplace, can be an explanation for the sector organization and for the importance attached or not to formal qualifications" (2008, p. 966).

Therefore, a broad and mostly undefined range of beliefs and feelings—dependent on the context, the culture, the sector, and the employers' values and experiences—affects the recruiting process, and an equally broad and undefined range affects "employability building" of the candidate.

Graduate recruitment and selection are based, in theory, upon "scientific" methods and techniques, in the effort to be as objective as possible. Despite this, in practice, most recruiters do not apply procedures and techniques as defined by methods (Knights and Raffo 1990).

Recruitment channels most popular in 1990 in the United Kingdom were annual "milk rounds" when recruiters reached candidates through universities,[9] recruitment brochures, recruitment fairs, direct directories, newspaper and magazine advertising, sponsorship, and recruitment agencies (Schofield 1991[10]). Afterwards, the internet became the preferred recruitment channel (Cappelli 2001), particularly in the United States and also in Europe (Sackett and Lievens 2008; Lievens et al. 2002; Gravili 2003 for Italy).

As regards selection, it seems acknowledged that "traditional" forms of selection based on psychometric techniques are not reliable anymore (Lievens et al. 2002). Traditional selection based on rather static professional profiles gave way to selection emphasising job analysis, criteria for assessing job performance, and prediction of work outcomes. Today, jobs have become ill-defined in a process that can be summarised as a "decline of jobs and emergence of work roles", and thus employees should be flexible in taking on different tasks and roles (Anderson and Herriot 1997). While there is no one universal selection process for winnowing the pool of candidates engaged through recruitment, the Table 5.2 offers a list of the common steps, how they were carried out traditionally, and how they are taken today:[11]

The process between educational achievement and the recruitment and selection process is directly linked to employability, as defined: being employable means being able to successfully navigate the recruitment processes and persuade the employer of one's "readiness" for work, a key concept.

Table 5.2 Trends in the selection process

Steps of selection	*Traditional selection*	*Today's selection*
Application	Collecting responses to job ads	In addition: • Qualifying questions in the application form • Gamification
CVs screening	Screening mostly based on background, it means on work experience	In addition: • Checking resumes' layout (e.g. creative; organised; catching; etc.) • Cover letter (convincing; engaging; precise; etc.) • Intangibles check (e.g. hobbies) • Managing recruiter's unconscious bias (related, e.g. to gender, race, etc.)
Screening call	Not common; more a call to schedule job interview	Short call to (try to) understand if the candidate is suitable and interested in the position, it is the first contact between the company and the applicant, and entails the following recruiter's steps: • Scheduling call; • Preparing basic and functional questions; • Exploring interests and expectations.
Assessment test	Assessment test, not always used; usually administered at the company (or recruiting agency) premises	Assessment test, not always used, can be administered: • At the company/recruiting agency premises; • Online test to explore personality, attitude, etc.; • Skills tests (e.g. speediness of typing)
In-person interviewing	Always face to face; questions are mostly related to educational credentials, previous work experiences, and expectations	Can be face to face, individual or in groups, or through audio-conferences. Questions usually include: • Job-related questions (role-specific; soft-skills; situational; behavioural); • Cultural fit questions (career goals, collaboration, adaptability)
Background checks	Related to administration mostly (criminal records; verification reports—e.g. credentials)	Also: checks can include drug tests, if applicable by national laws

(*continued*)

Table 5.2 (continued)

Steps of selection	*Traditional selection*	*Today's selection*
Reference checks	Checking references provided by candidates	Same as for traditional selection process
Decision and job offer	Job offer should be formulated first in person (or by phone), then in written form	Not very different from the traditional selection process, some differences in channels (e.g. the internet is mostly used to send the written proposal)

As for employability and employability skills, graduate work readiness is a relatively new concept and not yet clearly articulated. Some definitions include:

- "the extent to which graduates are perceived to possess the attitudes and attributes that make them prepared or ready for success in the work environment" (Cabellero and Walker 2010);
- "A 'work ready' individual possesses the foundational skills needed to be minimally qualified for a specific occupation as determined through a job analysis or occupational profile" (Clark et al. 2013);
- "a complex of generic attributes that allow graduates to apply their technical knowledge to problem-identification and problem-solving once they join the workforce" (Jollands et al. 2012);
- "enhanced capacity to ensure employment" (Glover et al. 2002);
- "component of the 'graduate-ness' (the effect on knowledge, skills and attitudes of having undertaken an undergraduate/graduate degree) of a student who has a sense of 'self-directedness,' or an ability to recognise one's 'personal agency' in obtaining and keeping employment" (Coetzee 2012).

These definitions of work readiness overlap and replace to some extent the concept of employability, and provide no consensus about the components of work readiness, or the ways to measure it (Prikshat et al. 2019b).

Although by now work readiness is part of higher education in the overall frame of an increased link between education and the labour market (Daniels and Broker 2014; Tynjälä et al. 2003), it is based on the business perspective, and emerged as a selection criterion for predicting graduate potential (Cabellero et al. 2011). Traditionally, selection of job candidates was based on academic (or technical) achievements; today, results from surveys and consultations indicate that more importance is given to the possession of a range of generic skills and attributes required across all jobs (Cabellero et al. 2011). The measurement of the work-readiness of graduates is more common in business settings. Several studies interviewed employers to identify the skills and preparation they deem to be components of work readiness (Casner-Lotto et al. 2006; Gardner and Liu 1997; Hart 2008; Stewart and Knowles 2000; Atlay and Harris 2000; and others).

Cabellero et al. (2011), developed the Work Readiness Scale (WRS) through qualitative research conducted with 30 HR professionals with experience in the recruitment and/or assessment of graduate job applicants. Based on their input, they developed the scale, then tested it with 251 graduates seeking employment. The qualitative data identified ten broad categories indicative of work readiness:

1. motivation
2. maturity
3. personal growth/development
4. organisational awareness
5. technical focus
6. interpersonal orientation
7. attitudes to work
8. problem-solving
9. adaptability
10. resilience

The ten broad categories informed the development of an initial 167 items, reduced to 64 items that were then piloted. Psychometric analysis indicated high reliability of four factors, namely labelled personal characteristics, organisational acumen, work competence, and social intelligence.

Prikshat et al. (2019a) modified the scale into the Work-Readiness Integrated Competence Model (WRICM), which consists of four main factors, namely intellectual, personality, meta-skill and job-specific resources, ten sub-dimensions, and 53 items covering work readiness skills. The scale was developed according to the inputs of 362 HR professionals and managers from seven Asia-Pacific countries. The authors define the GWR "as an integrated dynamic competence that requires the reconfiguration, synthesis and integration of four resources/

dimensions—namely, intellectual, personality, meta-skill and job-specific—that need to be channelled by graduates into a holistic, compelling and personal narrative that appeals to potential employers" (Prikshat et al. 2019b).

According to the authors, as a diagnostic tool, the WRICM can serve both educational and recruitment purposes; however, they acknowledge the limitation that the scale is based "largely on the perspectives of industry/employers" (Prikshat et al. 2019b).

In their efforts to ensure that the candidate is fit for the job and will be an added value for the company, recruiters use this and other tools that may differ in organisation and channels (e.g. group interviews vs individual interviews, or face-to-face interviews vs Skype interviews) and methods (e.g. behavioural interviews[12] or stress interviews[13]). In the "new economy" era, the idea that the graduate is the key to successful economic outcomes of organisations was summarised in the concept of "war for talent" (Michaels et al. 2001),[14] which refers to the increased competition in recruiting and retaining talented employees, who are the ones making the difference in knowledge-intensive businesses. In the first decade of the 2000s the "war for talent" was popular in discussions of recruiting practices,[15] even if the concept of "talent" had not been clearly defined, neither in the Michaels et al. book, nor in following publications. After the recent recession, the "war for talents" approach was abandoned, to some extent, as it was considered unfit for economic downturns.[16] Still, at least for managerial positions, which are seen as the most appropriate jobs for university graduates, the aim is to choose the candidate who can bring real added value to the company, because in a knowledge-based economy the individual is the key source of success. Do recruiters apply scientific methods in their assessment to identify the best candidate for this purpose? While recognising that assessment centres have brought a certain increase in objectivity to the recruitment processes, many scholars tend to doubt the scientific foundations of the process in practice. Many employers or recruiters use personality assessment tests to formulate interview questions (Branine 2008). Also, Brown and Hesketh (2004) point out that recruiters have their constructs in observing the data or in interviewing the candidate, so they interpret the data and reactions differently. Also, well-prepared candidates, the "Players", as Brown and Hesketh (2004) define them, know "the game" and can present themselves in such a way as to appear to be the best candidates.

5.4 Different Sizes and Different Needs? Large and Small Companies and Graduate Recruitment

Traditionally, employment opportunities for graduates have been provided by large enterprises (Branine 2008), but in recent years candidates have also been interested in SMEs, which are fully 99% of the businesses in Europe, providing around two-thirds of total employment (Eurostat 2019[17]). Studies of the graduate labour market in SMEs have explored only a few countries, in particular the United Kingdom (Ahmadi and Helms 1997; Holden and Jameson 2002; Holden et al. 2007; Hart and Barratt 2009; etc.). European studies form a smaller part of the literature on the topic, and are often limited to comparisons among countries (Manninen and Hobrough 2000; De Faoite et al. 2003).

Some characteristics of the topic of graduate employment in SMEs are common. On the one hand, "most SMEs do not perceive new graduates as a natural source of recruitment" (Westhead and Matlay 2005, p. 354), as they are too academic and lack basic business skills, or are too mobile, ready to leave for other opportunities (Roffe 1996; Westhead 1998; Szamosi 2006). On the other hand, graduates often consider SMEs to be a "second option" (Moy and Lee 2002), as medium- and large-sized companies with more than 100 employers offer better salaries and career development opportunities (Ahmadi and Helms 1997; Moy and Lee 2002).

SMEs have different recruiting channels than those of large companies. While a large company tends to apply the full process of recruitment and selection through internal or external recruiters, medium and particularly small companies tend to use more traditional recruiting methods, and look first at their networks.

Differences between large and SME management of recruiting, hiring, and managing the workforce could be summarised as in Table 5.3

Even though SMEs are generally reluctant to hire graduates, several studies have demonstrated the added value they bring to organisations in terms of performance (Sear et al. 2012), at least as increased productivity (Galindo-Rueda and Haskel 2005), innovation and growth (Lowden et al. Lowden et al. 2011; O'Brien and Clark 1997), skill levels (O'Brien and Clark 1997), management, leadership, and strategy (Holden et al. 2007).

Table 5.3 Recruiting, hiring and managing the workforce in large firms and SMEs

Dimension	*Large firms*	*SMEs*
Recruitment and selection	Application of complete recruitment and selection process, either carried out internally (HR unit) or externally (recruitment agency) (de Kok et al. 2011)	Tend to apply more traditional processes of recruiting and selection (in particular small enterprises <100 employees); smaller enterprises rely more on online job post publications and networking for recruiting purposes (de Kok et al. 2011; LinkedIn 2014); often apply informal channels (Barrett et al. 2007).
Earnings	Higher wages for the same role	Lower wages for the same role (Belfield 1998, p. 252; de Kok et al. 2011)
Work bargaining and fringe benefits	Common; performance payments and incentives are also common (de Kok et al. 2011)	Not common (Belfield 1998, p. 253)
Training	Formal training and training plans are common	Informal training more common than formal training
Internal labour market	Higher possibility of career within the company	Lower possibility of career within the company (Atkinson and Meager 1994)
Job quality and work environment	Indeterminate results: worsened as the size increase (Bryson et al. 2017)	Indeterminate results: worse work environment than larger firms de Kok et al. (2011, p. 135), better than in larger firms (Bryson et al. 2017)
Participation and representation	Very high (88% according to the de Kok et al. 2011, referring to EU data)	Rather low (34% according to the de Kok et al. 2011, referring to EU data)
Time flexibility	Common (de Kok et al. 2011)	Less common (it varies among countries, de Kok et al. 2011)
Job security	Stronger if compared to the risk of company death, but weaker for the extensive use of temporary agencies or fixed time contracts (de Kok et al. 2011)	Weaker if compared to the risk of company death, but stronger for the little use of temporary agencies, or fixed time contracts (de Kok et al. 2011)

5.5 Analysing Gaps in Transitions: The Concept of Skills Mismatch and the Role of Employers

In the analysis of the meso-level of employability, the "skills mismatch" also needs to be mentioned. This concept has been already outlined in the previous chapters: overeducation is an outcome of skills mismatch (vertical mismatch, the level of skills is less/more than required); and universities are asked to overcome the skills mismatch through curricula and teaching (horizontal mismatch, available skills are not needed in the market).

The ILO defines the skills mismatch as "an encompassing term which refers to various types of imbalances between skills offered and skills needed in the world of work".[18]

Countries of the European Union seem to be affected by high levels of skills mismatch, both vertical and horizontal: the New Skills Agenda (2016)[19] pointed out the about the 40% of employers had difficulties "in finding people with the skills they need to grow and innovate". The statement requires further attention, since it implies several levels of analysis.

First, skills mismatch depends on cyclical and structural factors (Brunello and Weuuk 2019). Cyclical factors depend on the economic flows; it means that during expansion, companies increase the demand for skills outside the labour market. Structural factors include demographics, in terms of both population ageing (differentiation of products and services' demand) and skills obsolescence (older workers). Most importantly, technological and digital transformation impacts skills shortages.

Second, the perception of skills shortages and mismatch also is based on determinants that do not depend directly on candidates' possessed skills. According to the CEDEFOP (2018), bottlenecks in recruiting include (quoted from page 42):

- Genuine skill shortage, as lack of applicants with the right skills and ability to offer a competitive starting salary.
- Apparent skill shortage, which includes lack of right skills and inability to offer a competitive starting salary by the company and lack of right skills and HRM inefficiency.
- Uncompetitive wage offer, as the inability to offer a competitive starting salary.
- HRM inefficiency, which includes both the lack of offer of competitive graduate training and development programme and a slow hiring process or limited resources to market vacancies.

In 2015, only 12% of companies with difficulties in filling vacancies had a genuine skills shortage, while 46% had an apparent skill shortage.

Finally, skills mismatch varies across sectors. The gap is higher for industries characterised by labour-intensive technologies and low innovative capabilities: for this reason, also, southern countries of Europe experience a low absorption of graduates (Meroni and Vera-Toscano 2017). One of the consequences is mobility; it happens from the South to the North of Europe, in southern countries also within the state, and in the regions, usually from rural to urban areas.

Notes

1. Deregulation started in these years in a few countries, such as the United Kingdom, while ten years later, in the 1990s, Italy and other countries began applying deregulation laws, or "flexibilisation of contracts".
2. The European social model envisions a society that combines economic growth with high living standards and good working conditions. It is often contrasted to the US liberal model.
3. Dual labour market is a wider concept that considers social issues, like gender or race, which cause a segmentation of labour. Here, the concept is used in the meaning introduced in 1971 by Doeringer and Piore as primary and secondary markets: it suggests that the labour market is divided into two segments, in which the first is characterized by "high wages, good working conditions, employment stability, chances of advancement, equity and due process in the administration of work rules", and the second by "low wages and fringe benefits, poor working conditions, high labour turnover, little chance of advancement, and often arbitrary and capricious supervision" (p. 165).
4. https://assets.publishing.service.gov.uk/government/uploads/system/uploads/attachment_data/file/746493/ESS_2017_UK_Report_Controlled_v06.00.pdf
5. https://www.weforum.org/reports/the-future-of-jobs-report-2018
6. https://excelsior.unioncamere.net/
7. http://ec.europa.eu/commfrontoffice/publicopinion/flash/fl_304_en.pdf
8. https://assets.publishing.service.gov.uk/government/uploads/system/uploads/attachment_data/file/746493/ESS_2017_UK_Report_Controlled_v06.00.pdf
9. Recruitment programme by which companies meet new graduates in universities.
10. The ranking is based on 153 interviews of graduate recruiters in the UK.

11. Sources: specialised websites, such as Workable; CareerBuilder; TrueCareers, BalanceCareers and books/guidelines, e.g. Arthur (2006).
12. Unlike traditional interviews, which are mostly focused on further exploring the information on the curriculum, behavioural interviews are aimed at understanding the candidates' reaction to specific cases they might have faced in past work experiences.
13. In stress interviews the recruiter tries to challenge the candidate (e.g. by being sarcastic or not empathetic) to see how the person reacts to stressful situations.
14. The term appeared the first time in a publication by McKinsey and Company in 1997.
15. Part of the "war of talent" discourse included discussions of "employer branding", the actions taken by a company to attract the best candidates (Barrow and Mosley 2005).
16. See *The War for Talent is First Casualty of the Crisis*, Financial Times, April 13, 2009
17. Retrieved online July 2019: https://ec.europa.eu/eurostat/statistics-explained/index.php/Statistics_on_small_and_medium-sized_enterprises#General_overview
18. https://unevoc.unesco.org/home/TVETipedia+Glossary/filt=all/id=568
19. https://ec.europa.eu/social/main.jsp?catId=1223

References

Ahmadi, M., & Helms, M. (1997). Small Firms, Big Opportunities: The Potential of Careers for Business Graduates in SMEs. *Education + Training, 39*(2), 52–57.

Anderson, N. R., & Herriot, P. (1997). Selecting for Change: How will Personnel and Selection Psychology Survive? In N. Anderson & P. Herriot (Eds.), *International Handbook of Selection and Assessment*. London: WileyEditors.

Archer, W., & Davison, J. (2008). *Graduate Employability: What Do Employers Think and Want?* London: The Council for Industry and Higher Education (CIHE).

Arthur, D. (2006). *Recruiting, Interviewing, Selecting & Orienting New Employees* (4th ed.). New York, NY: Arthur Associates Management Consultants, Ltd.

Atkinson, J. (1984). Manpower Strategies for Flexible Organisations. *Personnel Management, 16*, 28–31.

Atkinson, J., & Meager, N. (1994). Running to Stand Still. In J. Atkinson & D. Storey (Eds.), *Employment, the Small Firm, and the Labour Market*. London: Routledge.

Atlay, M., & Harris, R. (2000). An Institutional Approach to Developing Students' 'Transferable' Skills. *Innovations in Education & Training International, 37*(1), 76–84.

Bailly, F. (2008). The Role of Employers' Beliefs in the Evaluation of Educational Output. *Journal of Socio-Economics, 37*(3), 959–968.

Barrett, R., Neeson, R., & Billington, L. (2007). Finding the "Right Staff" in Small Firms. *Education + Training, 49*(8–9), 686–697.

Barrow, S., & Mosley, R. (2005). *The Employer Brand, Bringing the Best of Brand Management to People at Work*. Chichester, UK: John Wiley & Sons.

Becker, G. S. (1994). *Human Capital: A Theoretical and Empirical Analysis with Special Reference to Education*. Chicago: University Chicago Press. Retrieved from https://www.nber.org/books/beck94-1.

Belfield, C.R. (1998). The Behaviour of Graduates in the SME Labour Market: Evidence and Perceptions. *Small Business Economics, 12*, 249–259.

Branine, M. (2008). Graduate Recruitment and Selection in the UK. *Career Development International, 13*(6), 497–513.

Brown, P., & Hesketh, A. (2004). *The Mismanagement of Talent: Employability and Jobs in the Knowledge Economy*. Oxford: Oxford University Press.

Brunello, G., & Weuuk, P. (2019). *Skill Shortages and Skill Mismatch in Europe: A Review of the Literature*. Discussion Papers, IZA DP No. 12346. IZA-Institute of Labour Economics, Germany.

Bryson, A., Erhel, C., & Salibekyan, Z. (2017). *The Effects of Firm Size on Job Quality: A Comparative Study for Britain and France*. Department of Quantitative Social Science, Working Paper No. 17-08.

Cabellero, C., & Walker, A. (2010). Work Readiness in Graduate Recruitment and Selection: A Review of Current Assessment Methods. *Journal of Teaching and Learning for Graduate Employability, 1*(1), 13–25.

Cabellero, C. L., Walker, A., & Fuller-Tyszkiewicz, M. (2011). The Work Readiness Scale (WRS): Developing a Measure to Assess Work Readiness in College Graduates. *Journal of Teaching and Learning for Graduate Employability, 2*(2), 41–54.

Cappelli, P. (2001, March). Making the Most of Online Recruiting. *Harvard Business Review*, pp. 139–146.

Casner-Lotto, J., Barrington, L., & Wright, M. (2006). *Are They Really Ready to Work? Employers' Perspectives on the Basic Knowledge and Applied Skills of New Entrants to the 21st Century U.S. Workforce*. Research Report BED-06-Workforce. The Conference Board, Inc., Washington, DC, the Partnership for 21st Century Skills, Corporate Voices for Working Families, and the Society for Human Resources Management.

CEDEFOP (2013). *Piloting a European Employer Survey on Skill Needs. Illustrative Findings*. Luxembourg: Publications Office of the European Union.

CEDEFOP. (2018). *Insights Into Skill Shortages and Skill Mismatch: Learning from Cedefop's European Skills and Jobs Survey.* Luxembourg: Publications Office. Cedefop Reference Series; No 106.

Clark, H., LeFebvre, M., Burkum, K., & Kyte, T. (2013). *Work Readiness Standards and Benchmarks. The Key to Differentiating America's Workforce and Regaining Global Competitiveness.* Retrieved from https://files.eric.ed.gov/fulltext/ED546848.pdf.

Coetzee, M. (2012). A Framework for Developing Student Graduateness and Employability in the Economic and Management Sciences at the University of South Africa. In M. Coetzee, J.-A. Botha, N. Eccles, E. Nienaber, & N. Holtzhausen (Eds.), *Developing Student Graduateness and Employability: Issues, Provocations, Theory and Practical Guidelines* (pp. 119–152). Randburg: Knowres.

de Kok, J., Vroonhof, P., Verhoeven, W., Timmermans, N., Kwaak, T., Snijders, J. & Westhof, F. (2011). *Do SMEs Create More and Better Jobs?*. Brussels: EIM Business & Policy Research.

Daniels, J., & Brooker, J. (2014). Student Identity Development in Higher Education: Implications for Graduate Attributes and Work-readiness. *Educational Research, 56*(1), 65–76.

Davies, H. A., Csete, J., & Poon, L. K. (1999). Employers' Expectations of the Performance of Construction Graduates. *International Journal of Engineering Education, 15*(3), 191–198.

De Faoite, D., Henry, C., Johnston, K., & Van der Sijde, P. (2003). Education and Training for Entrepreneurs: A Consideration of Initiatives in Ireland and the Netherlands. *Education + Training, 45*(8), 430–438.

Doeringer, P. B., & Piore, M. J. (1971). *Internal Labour Markets and Manpower Analysis.* Lexington, MA: Heath Lexington Books.

European Commission (2016). *A New Skills Agenda for Europe.* Brussels: European Commission.

Eurostat (2019). Statistics on Small and Medium-sized Enterprises. *Eurostat Statistics Explained.* Authors: George Papadopoulos, Samuli Rikama, Pekka Alajääskö, Ziade Salah-Eddine (Eurostat, Structural business statistics), Aarno Airaksinen, Henri Luomaranta (Statistics Finland). https://ec.europa.eu/eurostat/statistics-explained/index.php/Statistics_on_small_and_medium-sized_enterprises#

Galindo-Rueda, F., & Haskel, J. (2005). *Skills, Workforce Characteristics and Firm Level Productivity: Evidence from the Matched ABI/Employer Skills Survey.* IZA Discussion Paper Series No. 1542. Retrieved October 04, 2012, from http://www.econstor.eu/bitstream/10419/21318/1/dp1542.pdf

Gallup Organization (2010). *Employers' Perception of graduate employability.* Survey conducted by The Gallup Organization, Hungary upon the request of

Directorate-General for Education and Culture. Flash EB Series #304. https://ec.europa.eu/commfrontoffice/publicopinion/flash/fl_304_en.pdf

Gardner, P. D., & Liu, W.-Y. (1997). Prepared to Perform? Employers Rate Work Force Readiness of New Grads. *Journal of Career Planning & Employment, 57*(3), 32–56.

Glover, D., Law, S., & Youngman, A. (2002). Graduateness and Employability: Student Perceptions of the Personal Outcomes of University Education. *Research in Post Compulsory Education, 7*(3), 293–306.

Gravili, G. (2003). Electronic Recruiting: Trends in the Italian Market. *EBS Review*, Autumn, Tallinn.

Hamilton, M., Carbone, A., Gonsalvez, C., & Jollands, M. (2015). *Breakfast with ICT Employers: What Do They Want to See in Our Graduates?* Proceedings of the 17th Australasian Computing Education Conference (ACE 2015), Sydney, Australia, 27–30 January 2015.

Hart, P. D. (2008). *How Should Colleges Assess and Improve Student Learning? Employers' Views on the Accountability Challenge, A Survey of Employers Conducted on Behalf Of: The Association of American Colleges and Universities.* Washington, DC: Peter D. Hart Research Associates, Inc.

Hart, T., & Barratt, P. (2009). The Employment of Graduates Within Small and Medium Sized Firms in England. *People, Place & Policy Online, 3*(1), 1–15.

Holden, R., & Jameson, S. (2002). Employing Graduates in SMEs: Towards a Research Agenda. *Journal of Small Business and Enterprise Development, 9*(3), 271–284.

Holden, R., Jameson, S., & Walmsley, A. (2007). New Graduate Employment Within SMEs: Still in the Dark? *Journal of Small Business and Enterprise Development, 14*(2), 211–227.

Jollands, M., Jolly, L., & Molyneaux, T. (2012). Project-based Learning as a Contributing Factor to Graduates' Work-Readiness. *European Journal of Engineering Education, 37*(2), 143–154.

Knights, D., & Raffo, C. (1990). Milkround Professionalism in Personnel Recruitment: Myth or Reality? *Personnel Review, 19*(1), 28–37.

Kranov, A. A., & Khalaf, K. (2016). *Investigating the Employment Gap: What Employers Want from Engineering Graduates.* 2016 IEEE Global Engineering Education Conference (EDUCON) Proceedings.

Levhari, D., & Weiss, Y. (1974). The Effect of Risk on the Investment in Human Capital. *The American Economic Review, 64*(6), 950–963.

Lievens, F., van Dam, K., & Anderson, N. (2002). Recent Trends and Challenges in Personnel Selection. *Personnel Review, 31*(5), 580–601.

LinkedIn Talent Solution (2014). *Insights Into How Small Businesses Hire.* LinkedIn Corporation.

Lowden, K., Hall, S., Elliott, D., & Lewin, J. (2011). *Employer Perceptions of the Employability Skills of New Graduates.* London: Edge Foundation.

Manninen, J., & Hobrough, J. (2000). Skills Gaps and Overflows? *Industry and Higher Education, 14*(1), 51–57.

Meroni, E. C., & Vera-Toscano, E. (2017). The Persistence of Overeducation Among Recent Graduates. *Labour Economics, 48*, 120–143.

Michaels, E., Handfield-Jones, H., & Axelrod, B. (2001). *The War for Talent.* Boston: Harvard Business Press.

Mourshed, M., Farrell, D., & Barton, D. (2012). *Education to Employment: Designing a System that Works.* McKinsey Centre for Government, McKinsey and Company.

Moy, J. W., & Lee, S. M. (2002). The Career Choice of Business Graduates: SMEs or MNCs? *Career Development International, 7*(6), 339–347.

O'Brien, E. M., & Clark, D. (1997). Graduates—Their Entrepreneurial Role in the Small Firm. *Marketing Education Review, 7*(3), 29–37.

Philips, K., & Eamets, R. (2007). *Approaches to Flexicurity: EU Models.* Luxembourg: European Foundation for the Improvement of Living and Working Conditions.

Prikshat, V., Kumar, S., & Nankervis, A. (2019a). Work-Readiness Integrated Competence Model: Conceptualisation and Scale Development. *Education + Training, 61*(5), 568–589.

Prikshat, V., Nankervis, A., Burgess, J., & Dhakal, S. (2019b). Conceptualising Graduate Work-Readiness: Theories, Concepts and Implications for Practice and Research. In S. Dhakal, V. Prikshat, A. Nankervis, & J. Burgess (Eds.), *The Transition from Graduation to Work. Challenges and Strategies in the Twenty-First Century Asia Pacific and Beyond.* Singapore: Springer Nature Pte Ltd.

Roffe, I. (1996). Transforming Graduates, Transforming Small Firms. *Journal of European Industrial Training, 20*(8), 3–9.

Sackett, P. R., & Lievens, F. (2008). Personnel Selection. *Annual Review of Psychology, 59*, 419–450.

Saunders, V., & Zuzel, K. (2010). Evaluating Employability Skills: Employer and Student Perceptions. *Bioscience Education, 15*(1), 1–15.

Schofield, P. (1991, January). The Difference a Graduate Recruitment Brochure can Make. *Personnel Management*, pp. 36–39.

Schultz, T. W. (1971). *Investment in Human Capital: The Role of Education and Research.* New York: The Free Press.

Sear, L., Scurry, T. Swail, J., & Down, S. (2012). *Graduate Recruitment to SMEs.* Department for Business, Innovation and Skills. SFEDI, Durham.

Spence, M. (1973). Job Market Signaling. *Quarterly Journal of Economics, 87*(3), 355–374.

Stewart, J., & Knowles, V. (2000). Graduate Recruitment and Selection Practices in Small Businesses. *Career Development International, 5*(1), 21–38.

Szamosi, L. T. (2006). Just What are Tomorrow's SME Employees Looking For? *Education + Training, 48*(8/9), 654–665.

Tangian, A. (2008). Is Europe Ready for flexicurity? Empirical Evidence, Critical Remarks and a Reform Proposal. *Intereconomics, 43*(2), 99–111.

Tynjälä, P., Välimaa, J., & Sarja, A. (2003). Pedagogical Perspectives on the Relationships between Higher Education and Working Life. *Higher Education, 46*(2), 147–166.

Valverde, M., Tregaskis, O., & Brewster, C. (2000). Labor Flexibility and Firm Performance. *International Advances in Economic Research, 6*, 649.

Westhead, P. (1998). The Shell Technology Enterprise Programme: Benefits Reported by Students and "Host" Employers. *Journal of Small Business and Enterprise Development, 5*(1), 60–78.

Westhead, P., & Matlay, H. (2005). Graduate Employment in SMEs: A Longitudinal Perspective. *Journal of Small Business and Enterprise Development, 12*(3), 353–365.

Wilthangen, T., & Tros, F. (2004). The Concept of "Flexicurity": A New Approach to Regulating Employment and Labour Markets. *Transfer, 10*(2), 166–186.

CHAPTER 6

Students and Graduates

Abstract This chapter addresses the micro-level of graduate employability, the level of the students and graduates. The concept of self-perceived employability is defined. Perception depends on aspects that include more than formal education: in particular, sociological research has advanced understanding of how the labour market, as a construct of individuals, is perceived subjectively by those preparing for or seeking work. Also, the perception of one's employability is conditioned by one's awareness of the global and the local labour markets, and of the channels to access work, which vary according to the work sector or type of company.

Keywords GenZ • Self-perceived employability • Transitions • Job seeking • Internships

6.1 The Most Educated Generations in History?

The generation of graduates accessing the labour market today, or those in the early stages of their professional careers, or finishing higher education, is commonly known as the Millennial generation[1] (but also Generation Y, Generation Next, or Generation Net). Some define Millennials as those born between 1981 and the mid-1990s, while others refer to the period 1980 to early 2000. In general, it can be said that Millennials are those reaching young adulthood in the twenty-first century.

G. Paviotti, *'Regional Universities' and Pedagogy*,
https://doi.org/10.1007/978-3-030-53680-0_6

Most of the literature on Millennials refers to data from the United States, where 22% of the population belongs to this generation. One of the primary references is the work of Strauss and Howe (2000), who were the first to identify common traits of the generation, listing seven main points (special, sheltered, confident, team-oriented, conventional, pressured, and achieving). Subsequent studies confirmed or refuted these initial assumptions, for example, insisting that Millennials are not team-oriented but individualistic (Twenge 2013), or condemning them as the "dumbest generation" (Bauerlein 2008). Still, all in all, at least in the US context, Millennials seem to be viewed as a generation with great potential. According to a PEW research elaboration (2018),[2] US Millennials are the most educated generation to date, as 21% of these men and 27% of these women have a college degree, while 18% and 20% respectively of the previous generation are college graduates.

In Europe, fewer studies and statistics have been conducted about Millennials, but some common qualities can be observed. In Europe, Millennials are the most educated generation so far, and women are more educated than their counterparts; they have grown up in a digital age and a globalised world. They form 20% of the population (Eurostat 2014), albeit with differences between countries, for example, Italy, where they represent the 15% of the population, and Spain, where they represent the 18.7%.

The demographic cohort following the Millennials is known as Generation Z, "the GenZ", the first "digital native" generation, the "Facebook Generation", and the "iGeneration" (Bencsik et al. 2016): these young people born from the mid-1990s to the early-2000s[3] are the present and near-future generation in higher education. The first comprehensive analysis of this cohort in the United States dates back to 2016, when Seemiller and Grace published their famous book *Generation Z Goes to College*. This study described members of this generation as 24/7 connected people, loyal, compassionate, thoughtful, open-minded, responsible, determined, committed to world's problems, socially liberal, and politically conservative, but mostly disengaged from political debate. They value education and believe that they need a university degree to access the labour market.

The university graduates of Generation Z in Europe are just beginning to enter the workforce and have not been studied in-depth, but some interesting findings are available. According to a survey of Generation Z members carried out by Universum[4] in 2015 (about 50,000 respondents across 46 countries), 67% of the sample (79% in Western Europe) felt that education choices should be based on interest in the subject. Asked about career goals, about 40% (rising to 50% in Eastern and Central Europe) indicated "a good work-life balance" and "being secure and stable in my job".[5] Features they looked for in a job were the opportunity to make an impact, to express creativity, and to be autonomous. Entrepreneurship was also indicated as a viable option. The respondents were not very optimistic about achieving a higher standard of living than their parents: while 71% of Millennials stated some optimism about this, only 56% of the Generation Z sample did. An additional and essential feature was the relationship with parents, who, according to 60% of the sample, influenced their decisions about education and career.

Both the Millennials and Generation Z shared a childhood marked by enormous and rapid changes in society and the economy that have lengthened the transition period from adolescence to adulthood, at least in comparison with previous generations. Young people in their 20s today do not perceive themselves as teens anymore, but neither do they regard themselves as adults. This phase, which takes place roughly between 18 and 25, was defined by Arnett in 2000 as "emerging adulthood", referring to the identity formation which emerges in adolescence. However, it is mostly developed later on, at least in industrialised societies. Work and career are part of identity formation: as pointed out by Konstam (2007), "emerging and young adults are potentially well-positioned to make informed career and personal decisions", since they have a "lengthened period of time to reach such key milestones as career, marriage, and parenthood in comparison to previous generations" (2007, p. 43). In this "good position", however, they deal with an unstable and unpredictable labour market and weakened labour protection. Moreover, as noted by Schulenberg et al. (2004):

> In comparing the transition into adolescence with the transition into adulthood, it becomes evident that there is far less institutionally and culturally imposed structure on young people as they make the latter transition than as they make the former transition. On the positive side, this relative lack of structure can allow for greater self-selection of paths and activities. [...] However, for some young people, the relatively sudden drop in institutional structure can be debilitating, creating a mismatch between individual needs and contextual affordances. (2004, p. 801)

During this phase of leaving behind adolescence and entering into young adulthood, young people choose their degree programs in tertiary education, shape their identity as professionals, build up their employability potential, and face the world of work.

6.2 Students and Employability

In the past few years, there has been an increased research on student perceptions about their employability (Jollands et al. 2012; Daniels and Brooker 2014; Smith et al. 2014; Tomlinson 2007; Taylor 2005). Individuals can shape their employability, referring to the labour market. If they do not have experience of it, as it often happens mainly with students at the beginning of their university studies, they refer to the construct of the labour market that they have built over the years in other settings. Frames of reference are always subjective (Tomlinson 2017): they depend on the person's relation with the social world, and incorporate subjectivities (influences and cultural practices over time), immediate social experiences (situations), and post-mediate experiences (how experiences are constituted) (Billett 1998). Over this, the understanding of the value of work contributes to the construct of the labour market. The meaning of work in social and cultural terms overcame the original sense of factor of production, and since the late nineteenth century has been conceived as a system for the distribution of income, rights, and welfare (Méda and Vendramin 2017, pp. 16–22). While in the first part of this century work was seen as a constituent of social cohesion, in the second part work has become an expression of self, shifting from the service to society to the individual self-fulfilment (Méda and Vendramin 2017). This value for society is also part of the students' life experience, and it influences first employability and then job search.

Self-perceived employability can be defined as the beliefs about the possibilities of obtaining stable employment. The concept has been recently formulated and has been explored through different stages of careers, from graduates to employees.

Among the numerous studies that investigated the topic and proposed scales to evaluate self-perceived employability, we focus on those more relevant for students and graduates. Evaluation of self-perceived employability could provide interesting elements for the university to assess their learning offer, and to students to reflect on their perceptions, also to plan following career development.

Rothwell et al. (2008) developed a 16-item scale for university students, designed around four quadrants:

- self-belief: graduates' engagement with their studies and academic performance (internal employability)
- my university: students' perception of the strengths of the university in terms of reputation (external employability)
- my field of studies: status of credibility of the graduates' field of study (external employability)
- external labour market: perception of the state of the labour market (external employability).

The questionnaire was administered to 315 students, who valued most external employability than internal employability items. The scale was further tested by other researchers (Vargas et al. 2018; Maiolo et al. 2013) and with additional elements (as career adaptability, Monteiro et al. 2018).

Following Rothwell et al. (2008) and Berntson et al. (2006) work, Qenani et al. (2014) proposed another questionnaire on self-perceived employability. Questions included human capital variables, satisfaction with how college provided students with the attributes needed for work, personality questions, perception of the state of the economy, and confidence about own employability. The questionnaire was administered to 978 students in two California colleges. Results included observation of a remarkable relationship between employment prospects and self-managing behaviour, the importance of internship for increasing self-perceived employability, and the significance of college reputation for students. Also, it found that gender plays a role: male students were 50% more confident on their employability skillset compared with female students.

Also, qualitative research was carried out on self-perceived employability. Tomlinson (2007, 2008) interviewed 55 undergraduates in their final year of studies and found that they had low expectations about the value of the degree to access the labour market. They recognised employability, however, as a "crucial issue which has to be negotiated and worked at", beyond the credential. Cavanagh et al. (2015) collected information through focus groups and interviews, concluding that there was a little capacity to link academic study with work activities in employability debates. A similar result has also been reported by Tymon (2013), following focus groups on a sample of over 400 students: undergraduates failed to understand the value of developing transversal skills through academic work and provided a narrow definition of employability, focused on access to employment. Instead, literature looks at that as a lifelong process that includes the overall professional career cycle.

Overall, it seems that what employability precisely means and how it is built during the study years vary across students' bodies. Research has explored the topic with different tools, and in different geographical, cultural, and institutional settings, that also probably affect perceptions. It would also be essential to continue work in this sense, to better understand how the assessment of own employability perception is constructed, and how to intervene to improve its potential, since transitions are far from being easy and smooth in the present labour markets.

6.3 Graduates' Transitions: Facing the Labour Market

The transition from education to work can be quite challenging: after years within a protected and linear system, young people face the increasing complexity of the adult world, including the world of work, and "sometimes they lose themselves in the process of transistion" (Sissors and Jones 2012; Smith et al. 2011).

The first real concern is to find a job. Traditionally, job search has been done using formal tools such as newspapers, offline or online job boards, and public and private employment services[6] and informal ones, such as social ties, social networks, and direct contact with employers (Wielgosz and Carpenter 1987; Try 2005). Several studies, mostly in the fields of economics and sociology, have investigated the efficacy and efficiency of those channels, in particular for public employment services, often in relation with national markets (Addison and Portugal 2001 in Portugal; Pagani 2003 in Italy). Reports in the literature suggest that informal job search methods are becoming increasingly effective. In contrast, other methods such as public employment services are used by job hunters "who cannot rely on social contacts" (Weber and Mahringer 2006). A survey from Right Management (Manpower Group 2010[7]) analysed data from 59,133 clients over three years, and found that in 2010, 41% of respondents landed a job through networking, 25% by following postings on internet job boards, and 11% through the services of agencies and search firms.

Since the 1960s, studies on paths to employment have stressed the role of personal networks or social ties in finding jobs (Rees 1966), and over the years this has been confirmed by other researchers (Wegener 1991; Holzer 1987; Wahba and Zenou 2005). With the advent of social networks, researchers have also studied the use of these tools for job hunting (Marin 2007; Cappellari and Tatsiramos 2015; Trimble and Kmec 2011; Trimble 2015).

Analysing social capital and its importance in finding and retaining work is, therefore, crucial for understanding access to work. The concept of networks relates to that of social capital. Bourdieu (1986) provided the first definition of social capital, as

> the aggregate of the actual or potential resources which are linked to possession of a durable network of more or less institutionalized relationships of mutual acquaintance and recognition—or in other words, to membership in a group—which provides each of its members with the backing of the collectively owned capital, a "credential" which entitles them to credit, in the various senses of the word. (1986, p. 21)

On the value of this capital, either economic, social, or cultural, Coleman (1988) argued that

> Social capital is defined by its function. It is not a single entity but a variety of different entities, with two elements in common: they all consist of some aspect of social structures, and they facilitate certain actions of actors—whether persons or corporate actors—within the structure. (1988, p. S98)

According to Portes (1998), there are "three basic functions of social capital: (a) as a source of social control; (b) as a source of family support; (c) as a source of benefits through extra-familial networks" (p. 10). Adler and Kwon (2002) also argue that networks have positive outcomes such as (a) information; (b) influence, control, and power; and (c) solidarity, but also can entail negative aspects, such as the demands on one's time, and the risk of being closed and self-referential.

Three main theoretical approaches can be considered for application to career and employment purposes:

- The theory of weak ties (Granovetter 1973).
- The structural hole theory (Burt 1992).
- The social resources theory (Lin 1990).

Granovetter (1973) held that "weak ties" with a social circle are more likely to connect job seekers to a job than "strong ties" with family and close friends, as the former provide broader access to information that can lead to increased opportunities. This theory is one of the most recognised and widely used ones in analysing access to work and career development.

Burt's (1992) structural holes approach focuses on the pattern of relations among the alters in an ego's social network, built on the main idea that lack of ties among alters (defined as "structural holes) may benefit ego.

Lin et al. (1981) focus on resources, viewing them as embedded in one's social network and social ties, which the individual can directly or indirectly access to fulfil the ego's instrumental objectives. Lin identifies three ways in which social networks enhance outcomes of action: the network facilitates the flow of information, influences the agents (e.g. recruiters), and certifies the individual's social credentials (Lin 1992).

Seibert et al. (2001) argued that differences between these conceptualisations are related to the distinction between structural properties of networks (the form, as weak ties and structural hole theories), and nature of social resources embedded in the same networks (as in social resources theory). They then proposed a model for a social capital theory of career success, where two measures of social network structures are related to two forms of social resources (number of contacts in other functions—weak ties—and number of connections at higher-educational level—structural holes). An additional measure refers to social resources, classified through three types of network benefits (access to information, access to resources, and career sponsorship). Their model was tested in a sample of 448 employees in various occupations and organisations, resulting in a confirmation that "the number of weak ties and the level of structural holes in an actor's network each has independent effects on the level of social resources" (page 15). Among the three types of network benefits, career sponsorship proved to be the most important in terms of career success.

Many other studies in a variety of academic fields focus on the value of social capital for the labour market, either for an organisation or an entrepreneur, or for the individual worker or jobseeker. Taking the personal perspective, we can broadly define three career stages in which social capital plays a role, although in different ways over time and in varying conditions:

(a) Access to the labour market.
(b) Staying within the labour market.
(c) Moving, voluntarily or not, from a job to another.

The second stage requires different actions concerning social capital, while the first and the third have in common the act of job seeking.

There is a considerable body of literature devoted to job hunting and its relation to social ties. Ioannides and Datcher Loury (2004), applied sociological theories in their economic perspective, and summarise seven "stylized facts" about job information networks, as follows (pp. 1057–1061):

1. there is widespread use of friends, relatives, and acquaintances to search for jobs and this has increased over time;
2. the use of friends and relatives to search for jobs often varies by location and by demographic characteristics (e.g. gender, education);
3. job search through friends and relatives is generally productive;
4. part of the variation in the productivity of job search by demographic group simply reflects differences in usage;
5. many differences in productivity of job search by age, gender, race, and ethnic group cannot be wholly accounted for by differences in usage;
6. the internet is being used increasingly for the purpose of job hunting; and
7. there appear to be significant differences across countries in the use of personal contacts by both firms and workers.

The authors approach the topic from economics, and provide an excellent review of available research on these "facts", considering mostly sources that rely on empirical quantitative data and economic modelling. As pointed out by Wright Brown and Konrad (2001), studies examining the use of personal contacts in the job search process were based on data sets collected between 15 and 30 years ago, when the labour market had remarkable differences from the present one. However, qualitative research confirms the listed "stylized facts".

The conscious use of networks for job hunting has increased over time (stylized fact 1, as in the list above), and is included in career development programmes. Grey literature, particularly the channels devoted to job hunting and recruitment through the internet (stylized fact 6), confirms that the use of networks for job-seeking purposes is considered valuable and relevant for success.

While social ties, networking, and other channels are used almost equally across Western countries by graduates to access their first job, the time needed to find it varies notably not only between the two sides of the Atlantic Ocean and Australia, but also within the countries of Europe. European surveys to study transition pathways of graduates are conducted at national levels, but some works have compared available national data. Among these, the CHEER project[8] in the late 1990s examined the relationships between higher education and the world of work in 11 European countries, highlighting similarities and differences among the nations studied. Analysing this dataset, Salas-Velasco (2007) investigated the entry into employment of young European graduates, concluding that:

- there is a gap between the North and the South of Europe, and graduates from Spain and Italy, for example, face more extended transition periods from university to obtain first job, compared to those from Nordic countries;
- job search intensity plays a role, where "graduates who search for a job more intensely increase the probability of finding a job sooner" (2007, p. 351);
- there is a critical gender difference that favours males;
- there is an age difference that supports younger graduates over mature graduates;
- parental education is a factor, as graduates from better-educated families are favoured in the process; and
- the type of degree is an important variable: for example, healthcare or computer science graduates are more likely to find a job in a shorter time than those with degrees in the humanities.

National studies in Spain (Lassibille et al. 2001), Italy (Almalaurea 2018), and Finland and Portugal (Alves and Korhonen 2016) have reached similar conclusions.

Finding a job, however, is only the first step. Then there is the process of integration into work settings. According to Graham and McKenzie (1995, p. 5), at least four critical issues should be considered when exploring transitions from education to work:

1. Culture change
2. Preparation of the graduates for the world of work
3. Expectations (of both graduates and employers)
4. Levels of commitment and satisfaction.

The first significant change is due to what has been called "reality shock" in nursing education (Kramer 1974) and "occupational reality shock" in accountancy (Lawler et al. 1975): every company has its own organisational culture. When graduates begin work, they find that they must not only learn about the firm's corporate arrangements and preferred communication styles, but also adopt beliefs and values perceived "as necessary for success" (Phillips 1987).

Preparation for the workplace is another issue. During work placements or internships, students experience the world of work, but from a "protected" position. Instead, as employees, the hard and soft skills acquired during their education are put to the test. Do graduates feel prepared? Most qualitative studies related to self-perception of readiness in graduates focus on specific professions, such as physicians or nurses. These studies delineate some role-specific difficulties as well as more general ones, such as the need to improve their communication skills (Robertson and Griffiths 2009) or a general feeling of unpreparedness for the role (Cave et al. 2009). Also, in engineering, the need for curricula improvements that help students develop generic or soft skills such as communication has been pointed out by some studies (Martin et al. 2005). General surveys in the grey literature confirm this perception of weak preparation for work, such as the totaljobs.com (2010)[9] survey in the United Kingdom, in which 44% of the 448 respondents said that university had not prepared them for the world of work.

The expectations of graduates and employers are generally divergent. Many studies in the literature have reported that the high expectations of graduates often end in disappointment with reality, in terms of salary (Hill 2002; Brunello and Lucifora 2001; Chevalier 2006 for gender differences), the feeling of being underutilised and burdened by heavy workloads (Holden and Jameson 1999), difficulties with organisational behaviour and culture (O'Reilly et al. 1991), or impediments to career progression (O'Leary and Deegan 2005; Erickson 2009; Pooley 2005). As outlined in the previous chapter, employers expect their new hires to be ready for the job, able "to start making a contribution from 'Day 2'" (Graham and McKenzie 1995, p. 7).

Finally, two critical and related elements of the transition from studies to work are commitment and job satisfaction. These factors have been widely studied. Graham and McKenzie (1995) examined the level of satisfaction of about 2000 graduates in more than 15 UK organisations one to three years after beginning their job, and identified five patterns among the sample:

- *Success*: graduates happy in their role
- *The W*: graduates alternating between periods of high satisfaction and high dissatisfaction
- *Acceptance and underutilisation*: graduates accepting that they will not utilise their talents, with a resigned attitude
- *Steady decline*: graduates acknowledging and expecting to leave the company after a time (this was the most represented pattern)
- *Shock and recovery*: graduates feeling very insecure at the beginning of their work, who then became firmly committed to the organisation.

Commitment and satisfaction depend on many aspects beyond company management and organisation: these also impact the patterns explained above. The study by Mora et al. (2007), again based on the CHEER database, explored job satisfaction across 11 European countries, finding that

- job satisfaction among very different European countries is relatively homogeneous, and national results do not differ substantially from overall results;
- men tend to be more satisfied than women, also considering that women have more inadequate jobs and struggle more to reconcile work and family;
- graduates who had practical experiences during their educational journey tend to be more satisfied;
- positions gained generally do not correspond to expectations, in terms of earnings;
- over-qualification is the first reason for dissatisfaction;
- more job satisfaction is encountered in the public sector, particularly in education, and in small firms;
- job satisfaction is higher in a permanent and full-time job; and
- a good salary is a key factor for increased job satisfaction.

Finally, to better understand the transition to the labour market and placement in a (hopefully satisfactory) job, it is useful to consider the time needed to get the first significant job[10] and the terms of the contract. The time required to find a first job varies among European countries from the 2.6 months needed for a graduate in Malta to the 12.2 months in Greece (Eurostat 2009—last available data). The different length depends on several factors, including the general employment rate of the country.

Economic performance of the single countries is not the only reason, as Salas-Velasco (2007) noted. The OECD study on transitions (2000) points out six "key ingredients of successful transition systems": "a healthy economy; well-organised pathways that connect initial education with work and further study; widespread opportunities for workplace experience to be combined with education; tightly knit safety nets for those at risk; good information and guidance; and effective institutions and processes" (2000, p. 13). Raffe (2011) argues that different types and lengths of transition depend on internal "logics" within countries, influenced by different welfare regimes, family support structures, the existence of extensive work-based learning practices during educational pathways, and other factors. Raffe concluded that there is no one overarching transition model, and no convergence among countries that could lead to one in a short time.

Another element that both the OECD study and Raffe underline is the increased disadvantage of young people in relation to older workers, as the "losers in the globalization process" (Buchloz et al. 2009, p. 67). Young people face greater instability in the labour market and decreased labour protections, and their employment is mainly temporary (when not precarious, in some countries). Statistical data highlight that temporary contracts across Europe range from the 56.1% of France to the 2.7% of Slovakia (Eurostat 2018[11]). An average of 30% of young people in the European Union have "involuntary part-time"[12] contracts. Still, this average is based on substantial discrepancies: 8.4% of young workers in the Netherlands have such agreements, compared to fully 80% in Italy.[13] Involuntary part-time jobs are part of an overall precariousness of the labour market, particularly in some countries like Italy or Spain, where labour contracts proposed to young people are often atypical.[14] The impact of precarious job conditions is relevant on both society and individuals. In the words of Standing (2011), a "new class", the Precariat, lives a precarious existence of persistent job insecurity. Such job insecurity can cause increased stress levels (Büssing 1999), depression (Meltzer et al. 2010), and poor health in general (László et al. 2010). Besides, the first years in professional settings in precarious job conditions often lead to the "scarring effect", defined as "effects of youth unemployment over the working life, as more spells of unemployment, lower earnings prospects and lower chances of obtaining a decent job in the longer term"[15] (Gregg and Tominey 2005; Mroz and Savage 2006).

Having all this in mind, we should then reconsider employability narratives from several points of view: to gain credentials, to have acquired relevant skills, is definitely not enough, echoing Tomlinson (2007). Transitions were hard when the labour market was stable. Today, transitions also suffer from intrinsic conditions of the labour market: this impacts particularly some countries of Europe, for structural economic reasons, but anyway affects all the youth cohorts more than older generations across the continent.

6.4 Internships and Traineeships

Within precarious job conditions, it is worth to separately mention internships and traineeships, which are considered by some graduates as "jobs" as they sometimes provide a minimum income. This phenomenon is quite recent, and it does not affect equally the countries of Europe.

Internships and traineeships can have unclear definitions when translated into other languages from English and applied to national contexts. For clarity, here we take the EURES meanings:[16] internship is a work experience carried out while studying, and it is often curricular (needed to complete the study course); traineeship is a work practice, which is usually carried out after the end of the studies to gain some work experience. Traineeship can be paid or unpaid and has (or should have) a learning component. It should be stressed, however, that the most used word, also in associations fighting against the abuse of those tools in the labour market, is "internships" ("Internship Generation").

Both instruments have an enormous added value for both students and graduates: internships allow to practice, to get experience of a business environment, and also to understand if the professional profile is in reality what students have imagined. Traineeship can be a useful step in the beginning of the professional career, as a job insertion tool, and allows the trainee to gain work experience that is valued in the curriculum. The first takes place under the supervision of the university. The second, instead, is usually based on the agreement between the company and the trainee.

Across Europe, particularly traineeships have been subject to misconduct in job relations: in 2016, the Eurofound indicated this traineeships as a type of fraudulent contracting of work. Causes for the abuse of this type of instrument have been identified as lower labour cost, since often there are no social contribution or taxes due, and higher flexibility, as traineeships have a short duration (usually up to six months). The improper use of the instrument also has social and economic consequences, such as unfair competition, low health and safety on the job, and missed contributions to states' taxes and social security systems. Here we focus on consequences on the individuals, since the phenomenon remarkably affects even graduates in many countries. According to a literature review carried out by Cerulli-Harms (2017, pp. 4–6), the negative impact of traineeships (called internships) includes signals in employers, who can look at the interns as "negative selection among graduates"; locking-in effects, as the job-search intensity is decreased during the traineeship; scarring effects, for both the need of finding an income (also low), and the risk of being considered an "eternal intern" afterwards. The opportunity for learning on the job and gain some experience, then, risks becoming a trap: national and transnational associations and NGOs were founded to fight the practice of unpaid traineeship with no learning content. The European Commission survey (2013) reported that at least 30% fall into this category; also, the 59% of traineeships are unpaid, and 40% have no regular agreement. Graduates composed 61% of the sample.

Political intervention and strict rules are needed to be incorporated in regulations on the number of traineeships that an individual can undergo. It could happen, therefore, that the graduate, in our case, falls in a sort of "internship trap", passing from one to another, postponing the access to regular employment contracts. In past years, both the European Union (2014) and the International Labour Organisation (2018) have addressed this issue.

Notes

1. The term is accredited to Strauss and Howe (2000).
2. https://www.pewresearch.org/fact-tank/2018/03/16/how-millennials-compare-with-their-grandparents/ft_millennials-education_031715/
3. According to Pew Research Generation Z is from 1997 to 2012 (https://www.pewresearch.org/fact-tank/2019/01/17/where-millennials-end-and-generation-z-begins/); following Seemiller and Grace (2016), the same gathers born between 1995 and 2010.

4. https://universumglobal.com/product/generation-z-grows/
5. Also, Seemiller and Grace (2016) point out this characteristic, which might depend on the fact that this generation saw their parents struggling for jobs during the economic crisis.
6. Job search theories have been popular since the 1970s, replacing the neo-classical labour supply theory, which was based on the assumption that there was no way for anyone actively looking for a job to remain jobless; therefore, the individual could be employed or inactive—unemployment was not included. Job search models are based on the assumption that "looking for a job is a dynamic sequential process and that individuals have to decide when to stop this process under conditions of uncertainty and imperfect information. Frictional unemployment is a natural outcome of this process" (Faggian 2014, p. 60).
7. https://www.forbes.com/sites/susanadams/2011/06/07/networking-is-still-the-best-way-to-find-a-job-survey-says/#21b5dd1a4366
8. https://www.qtafi.de/cheers-european-graduate-survey.html. The study included surveys in Austria, the Czech Republic, Finland, France, Germany, Italy, the Netherlands, Norway, Spain, Sweden, and the UK.
9. https://www.totaljobs.com/
10. "Significant job" refers to a work contract for at least three months in the Eurostat surveys after 2009 (Eurostat 2015); the previous definition was based on a contract of at least six months (European Union Labour Force Survey 2000).
11. Eurostat table "Young temporary employees as percentage of the total number of employees, by country of birth [yth_empl_050], age class: 15-29"
12. Involuntary part-time employment refers to those who work part-time because they could not find full-time work (Eurofound 2016).
13. Eurostat table [yth_empl_080]: Involuntary part-time employment as percentage of the total part-time employment for young people by sex and age https://appsso.eurostat.ec.europa.eu/nui/show.do?dataset=yth_empl_080&lang=en
14. "Atypical work refers to employment relationships that do not conform to the standard or 'typical' model of full-time, regular, open-ended employment with a single employer over a long time span. [...] Atypical work includes part-time work, temporary work, fixed-term work, casual and seasonal work, self-employed people, independent workers and home workers. Although the number of workers in non-standard employment has grown significantly over the past two decades, these workers continue to be regarded as being in 'atypical' employment" (Eurofound, https://www.eurofound.europa.eu/observatories/eurwork/industrial-relations-dictionary/atypical-work).

15. https://www.igi-global.com/dictionary/youth-employment/59265
16. https://ec.europa.eu/eures/public/news-articles/-/asset_publisher/L2ZVYxNxK11W/content/traineeship-internship-apprenticeship-which-one-is-for-you-?_101_INSTANCE_L2ZVYxNxK11W_backLabelKey=news.articles.back.to.list&_101_INSTANCE_L2ZVYxNxK11W_showAssetFooter=true

References

Adams, S. (2011). Networking Is Still The Best Way To Find A Job, Survey Says. Forbes, Jun 7, 2011 Note/website https://www.forbes.com/sites/susanadams/2011/06/07/networking-is-still-the-best-way-to-find-a-job-survey-says/#21b5dd1a4366

Addison, J., & Portugal, P. (2001). *Job Search Methods and Outcomes.* IZA Discussion Papers 349. Retrieved from https://www.econstor.eu/bitstream/10419/21208/1/dp349.pdf

Adler, P., & Kwon, S. (2002). Social Capital: Prospects for a New Concept. *The Academy of Management Review, 27*(1), 17–40.

Almalaurea. (2018). *XX Indagine—Condizione occupazionale dei Laureati.* Bologna: Consorzio Almalaurea.

Alves, M. G., & Korhonen, V. (2016). Transitions and Trajectories from Higher Education to Work and Back—A Comparison between Finnish and Portuguese Graduates. *European Educational Research Journal, 15*(6), 676–695.

Annual Population Survey. (2018). *Understanding Society: The UK Household Longitudinal Study. Young People's Perceptions of the Labour Market (2015-16-17).* UK Office for National Statistics.

Arnett, J. J. (2000). Emerging Adulthood. A Theory of Development From the Late Teens Through the Twenties. *American Psychologist, 55*(5), 469–480.

Bauerlein, M. (2008). *The Dumbest Generation: How the Digital Age Stupefies Young Americans and Jeopardizes Our Future (Or, Don't Trust Anyone Under 30).* New York: Jeremy P. Tarcher and Penguin.

Bencsik, A., Horváth-Csikós, G., & Juhász, T. (2016). Y and Z Generations at Workplaces. *Journal of Competitiveness, 8*(3), 90–106.

Berntson, E., & Marklund, S. (2007). The Relationship between Perceived Employability and Subsequent Health. *Work and Stress, 21*(3), 279–292.

Berntson, E., Sverke, M., & Marklund, M. (2006). Predicting Perceived Employability: Human Capital or Labour Market Opportunities? *Economic and Industrial Democracy, 27*(2), 223–244.

Billett, S. R. (1998). Situation, Social Systems and Learning. *Journal of Education and Work, 11*(3), 255–274.

Bourdieu, P. (1986). The Forms of Capital. In J. Richardson (Ed.), *Handbook of Theory and Research for the Sociology of Education* (pp. 241–258). Westport, CT: Greenwood.

Brown, D. W., & Konrad, A. M. (2001). Job-Seeking in a Turbulent Economy: Social Networks and the Importance of Cross-industry Ties to an Industry Change. *Human Relations, 54*(8), 1015–1044.

Brunello, G., & Lucifora, C. (2001). *The Wage Expectations of European College Students.* IZA Discussion Papers No. 299. Retrieved from https://www.econstor.eu/bitstream/10419/21153/1/dp299.pdf

Buchloz, S., Hofacker, D., Mills, M., Blossfeld, H.-P., Kurz, K., & Hofmeister, H. (2009). Life Courses in the Globalization Process: The Development of Social Inequalities in Modern Societies. *European Sociological Review, 25*(1), 53–71.

Burt, R. (1992). *Structural Holes: The Social Structure of Competition.* Boston, MA: Harvard Press.

Büssing, A. (1999). Can Control at Work and Social Support Moderate Psychological Consequences of Job Insecurity? Results from a Quasi-experimental Study in the Steel Industry. *European Journal of Work and Organizational Psychology, 8*(2), 219–242.

Cappellari, L., & Tatsiramos, K. (2015). With a Little Help from My Friends? Quality of Social Networks, Job Finding and Job Match Quality. *European Economic Review, 78*, 55–75.

Cavanagh, J., Burston, M., Southcombe, A., & Bartram, T. (2015). Contributing to a Graduate-Centred Understanding of Work Readiness: An Exploratory Study of Australian Undergraduate Students' Perceptions of Their Employability. *The International Journal of Management Education, 13*, 278–288.

Cave, J., Woolf, K., Jones, A., & Dacre, J. (2009). Easing the Transition from Student to Doctor: How can Medical Schools Help Prepare Their Graduates for Starting Work? *Medical Teacher, 31*(5), 403–408.

Cerulli-Harms, A. (2017). *Generation Internship: The Impact of Internships on Early Labour Market Performance.* IZA Discussion Papers, No. 11163. Institute of Labor Economics (IZA), Bonn.

Chevalier, A. (2006). *Education, Occupation and Career Expectations: Determinants of the Gender Pay Gaps in UK Graduates.* London, UK: London School of Economics. Retrieved from https://files.eric.ed.gov/fulltext/ED530654.pdf.

Coleman, J. S. (1988). Social Capital in the Creation of Human Capital. *The American Journal of Sociology, 94*, S95–S120.

Daniels, J., & Brooker, J. (2014). Student Identity Development in Higher Education: Implications for Graduate Attributes and Work-Readiness. *Educational Research, 56*(1), 65–76.

Erickson, T. J. (2009, February). Gen Y in the Workforce: How I Learned to Love Millennials and Stop Worrying about What They are Doing with Their iPhones. *Harvard Business Review*.

Eurofound. (2016). *Exploring the Fraudulent Contracting of Work in the European Union*. Luxembourg: Publications Office of the European Union.

European Commission. (2013). *The Experience of Traineeship in the EU*. Flash Eurobarometer 378.

European Union. (2014). *Council Recommendation of 10 March 2014 on a Quality Framework for Traineeships*. Official Journal of the European Union C 88/1, 27.3.2014.

Eurostat (2000). *European Union Labour Force Survey (EU-LFS)*. Brussels: Eurostat Statistics Explained.

Eurostat (2009). *Table edat_lfso_09t2. Average time between leaving formal education and starting the first job by age, sex and educational attainment level for persons who left within the last 3 or 5 years - (months)*. Brussels: Eurostat.

Eurostat (2014). *Population and Population Change Statistics*. Brussels: Eurostat Statistics Explained Eurostat (2014). Population and population change statistics. Brussels: Eurostat Statistics Explained.

Eurostat (2015). *School-to-Work Transition Statistics*. Statistic Explained. Web publication: https://ec.europa.eu/eurostat/statistics-explained/index.php/Archive:School-to-work_transition_statistics#:~:text=In%20the%20EU%2C%20the%20average,2009%20for%20all%20educational%20levels. (last update 12 June 2015).

Eurostat (2018). *Table yth_empl_050. Young temporary employees as percentage of the total number of employees, by country of birth age class: 15–29*. Brussels: Eurostat.

Faggian, A. (2014). Job Search Theory. In M. M. Fischer & P. Nijkamp (Eds.), *Handbook of Regional Science*. Berlin: Springer.

Graham, C., & McKenzie, A. (1995). Delivering the Promise: The Transition from Higher Education to Work. *Education + Training, 37*(1), 8.

Granovetter, M. (1973). The Strength of Weak Ties. *American Journal of Sociology, 78*(6), 1360–1380.

Granovetter, M. (1974). *Getting a Job: A Study of Contacts and Careers*. Cambridge, MA: Harvard University Press.

Gregg, P., & Tominey, E. (2005). The Wage Scar from Male Youth Unemployment. *Labour Economics, 12*(4), 487–509.

Hill, R. P. (2002). Managing Across Generations in the 21st Century: Important Lessons from the Ivory Trenches. *Journal of Management Inquiry, 11*, 60–66.

Hillage, J., & Pollard, E. (1998). *Employability: Developing a Framework for Policy Analysis*. London: Institute for Employment Studies.

Holden, R. J., & Jameson, S. M. (1999). A Preliminary Investigation Into the Transition and Utilization of Hospitality Graduates in SMEs. *Tourism and Hospitality Research, 1*(3), 231–242.
Holzer, H. J. (1987). Informal Job Search and Black Youth Unemployment. *American Economic Review, 77*, 446–452.
International Labour Office—ILO. (2018). *The Regulation of Internships. A Comparative Study*. Employment Working Paper No. 240. ILO, Geneva.
Ioannides, Y. M., & Datcher Loury, L. (2004). Job Information Networks, Neighborhood Effects, and Inequality. *Journal of Economic Literature., 42*(4), 1056–1093.
Jollands, M., Jolly, L., & Molyneaux, T. (2012). Project-based Learning as a Contributing Factor to Graduates' Work-Readiness. *European Journal of Engineering Education, 37*(2), 143–154.
Konstam, V. (2007). *Emerging and Young Adulthood: Multiple Perspectives, Diverse Narratives*. New York: Springer.
Kramer, M. (1974). *Reality Shock: Why Nurses Leave Nursing*. St Louis: C.V. Mosby Company.
Lassibille, G., Navarro, L., Aguilar, I., & Sanchez, C. (2001). Youth Transition from School to Work in Spain. *Economics of Education Review, 20*, 139–149.
László, K. D., Pikhart, H., Kopp, M. S., Bobak, M., Pajak, A., Malyutina, S., Salavecz, G., & Marmot, M. (2010). Job Insecurity and Health: A Study of 16 European Countries. *Social Science & Medicine, 70*(6), 867–874.
Lawler, E. E., Kuleck, W. J., Rhode, J. G., & Sorensen, J. E. (1975). Job Choice and Post Decision Dissonance. *Organizational Behavior and Human Performance, 13*, 133–145.
Lin, N. (1990). Social Resources and Social Mobility: A Structural Theory of Status Attainment. In R. Breiger (Ed.), *Social Mobility and Social Structure*. New York: Cambridge University Press.
Lin, N. (1992). Social Resources Theory. In E. F. Borgatta & L. Marie (Eds.), *Encyclopedia of Sociology* (Vol. 4, pp. 1936–1942). Borgatta, NY: Macmillan.
Lin, N., & Dumin, M. (1986). Access to Occupations Through Social Ties. *Social Networks, 8*(4), 365–385.
Lin, N., Ensel, W. M., & Vaughn, J. C. (1981). Social Resources and Strength of Ties: Structural Factors in Occupational Status Attainment. *American Sociological Review, 46*(4), 393–405.
Maiolo, M., Zuffo, R. G., & Cortini, M. (2013). Students' Academic Performance and Employability A Study on Italian Undergraduates. *International Journal of Learning in Higher Education, 19*(4), 49–60.
Manpower Group (2010). *Right Management Global Survey Report 2010*.
Marin, A. (2007). *Social Capital as Process: The Network Sources of Latent, Available, and Accessed Job Information*. (PhD dissertation). Department of Sociology, Harvard University, Cambridge, MA.

Martin, R., Maytham, B., Case, J., & Fraser, D. (2005). Engineering Graduates' Perceptions of How Well They were Prepared for Work in Industry. *European Journal of Engineering Education, 30*(2), 167–180.

Méda, D., & Vendramin, P. (2017). *Reinventing Work in Europe. Value, Generations and Labour*. London, UK: Palgrave Macmillan.

Meltzer, H., Bebbington, P., Brugha, T., Jenkins, R., McManus, S., & Stansfeld, S. (2010). Job Insecurity, Socio-economic Circumstances and Depression. *Psychological Medicine, 40*, 1401–1407.

Monteiro, S., Ferreira, J. A., & Almeida, L. S. (2018). Self-perceived Competency and Self-perceived Employability in Higher Education: The Mediating Role of Career Adaptability. *Journal of Further and Higher Education, 42*, 1–15.

Mora, J., Garcia, A., Garcia-Aracil, A., & Vila, L. E. (2007). Job Satisfaction Among Young European Higher Education Graduates. *Higher Education, 53*, 29–59.

Mroz, T. A., & Savage, T. H. (2006). The Long-Term Effects of Youth Unemployment. *Journal of Human Resources, 41*(2), 259–293.

O'Leary, S., & Deegan, J. (2005). Career Progression of Irish Tourism and Hospitality Management Graduates. *International Journal of Contemporary Hospitality Management, 17*(5), 421–432.

O'Reilly, C. A., Chatman, J., & Caldwell, D. F. (1991). People and Organizational Culture: A Profile Comparison Approach to Assessing Person-Organization Fit. *Academy of Management Journal, 34*(3), 487–516.

OECD. (2000). *From Initial Education to Working Life: Making Transitions Work*. Paris: OECD.

Pagani, L. (2003). Why Do People from Southern Italy Seek Jobs in the Public Sector? *LABOUR, 17*(1), 63–91.

Phillips, J. (1987). *Recruiting, Training and Retraining New Employees*. New York, NY: Jossey-Bass.

Pooley, E. (2005). Generation Y: How Twenty Somethings are Changing the Workplace. *Canadian Business*, p. 6.

Portes, A. (1998). Social Capital: Its Origins and Applications in Modern Sociology. *Annual Review of Sociology, 24*, 1–24.

Qenani, E., MacDougall, N., & Sexton, C. (2014). An Empirical Study of Self-perceived Employability: Improving the Prospects for Student Employment Success in an Uncertain Environment. *Active Learning in Higher Education, 15*(3), 199–213.

Raffe, D. (2011). Cross-National Differences in Education-Work Transitions. In M. London (Ed.), *The Oxford Handbook of Lifelong Learning* (pp. 312–328). New York: Oxford University Press.

Rees, A. (1966). Information Networks in Labor Markets. *The American Economic Review, 56*(1/2), 559–566.

Robertson, L. J., & Griffiths, S. (2009). Graduates' Reflections on Their Preparation for Practice. *British Journal of Occupational Therapy, 72*(3), 125–132.

Rogoff, B. (1995). Observing Sociocultural Activity on Three Planes: Participatory Appropriation, Guided Participation, and Apprenticeship. In J. V. Wertsch, P. del Río, & A. Alvarez (Eds.), *Sociocultural Studies of Mind*. New York: Cambridge University Press.

Rothwell, A., & Arnold, J. (2007). Self-perceived Employability: Development and Validation of a Scale. *Personnel Review, 36*(5), 23–41.

Rothwell, A., Herbert, I., & Rothwell, F. (2008). Self-Perceived Employability: Construction and Initial Validation of a Scale for University Students. *Journal of Vocational Behavior, 73*(1), 1–12.

Salas-Velasco, M. (2007). The Transition from Higher Education to Employment in Europe: The Analysis of the Time to Obtain the First Job. *Higher Education, 54*(3), 333–360.

Schulenberg, J. E., Sameroff, A. J., & Cicchetti, D. (2004). The Transition to Adulthood as a Critical Juncture in the Course of Psychopathology and Mental Health. *Development and Psychopathology, 16*, 4.

Seemiller, C., & Grace, M. (2016). *Generation Z Goes to College*. San Francisco, CA: Jossey-Bass.

Seibert, S. E., Kraimer, M. L., & Liden, R. C. (2001). A Social Capital Theory of Career Success. *Academy of Management Journal, 44*(2), 219–237.

Sissors, S., & Jones, K. (2012). *Lost in Transition? The Changing Labour Market and Young People Not in Employment, Education or Training*. The Work Foundation.

Smith, C., Christoffersen, W., Davidson, H., & Snell Herzog, P. (2011). *Lost in Transition. The Dark Side of Adulthood*. New York: Oxford University Press.

Smith, C., Ferns, S., & Russell, L. (2014). Conceptualising and Measuring "Employability": Lessons from a National OLT Project. In *ACEN National Conference* (pp. 1–10). Gold Coast: Australian Collaborative Education Network Limited.

Smith, V. (2016). Employment Uncertainty and Risk. In S. Edgell, H. Gottfried, & E. Granter (Eds.), *The SAGE Handbook of Sociology of Work and Employment*. London: SAGE Publications Ltd..

Smykal, E. (2016). *Flexible Jobs: How the Gig Economy is Impacting Recruiting*. Aurora: Talent Acquisition Excellence Essentials.

Standing, G. (2011). *The Precariat. The New Dangerous Class*. Bloomsbury.

Strauss, W., & Howe, N. (2000). *Millennials Rising: The Next Great Generation*. Cartoons by R. J. Matson. New York: Vintage Original.

Taylor, A. (2005). What Employers Look For: The Skills Debate and the Fit with Youth Perceptions. *Journal of Education and Work, 18*(2), 201–218.

Tomlinson, M. (2007). Graduate Employability and Student Attitudes and Orientations to the Labour Market. *Journal of Education and Work, 20*(4), 285–304.

Tomlinson, M. (2008). 'The Degree is Not Enough': Students' Perceptions of the Role of Higher Education Credentials for Graduate Work and Employability. *British Journal of Sociology of Education, 29*(1), 49–61.

Tomlinson, M. (2017). Forms of Graduate Capital and Their Relationship to Graduate Employability. *Education + Training, 59*(4), 338–352.

Trimble, L. (2015). Ask and You Shall Receive: Social Network Contacts' Provision of Help During the Job Search. *Social Networks, 35*, 593–603.

Trimble, L. B., & Kmec, J. A. (2011). The Role of Social Networks in Getting a Job. *Sociology Compass, 5*, 165–178.

Try, S. (2005). The Use of Job Search Strategies Among University Graduates. *The Journal of Socio-Economics, 34*, 223–243.

Twenge, J. M. (2013). The Evidence for Generation Me and Against Generation We. *Emerging Adulthood, 1*(1), 11–16.

Tymon, A. (2013). The Student Perspective on Employability. *Studies in Higher Education, 38*(6), 841–856.

Vargas, R., Sánchez-Queija, M. I., Rothwell, R., & Parra, Á. (2018). Self-perceived Employability in Spain. *Education + Training, 60*(3), 226–237.

Wahba, J., & Zenou, Y. (2005). Density, Social Networks and Job Search Methods: Theory and Application to Egypt. *Journal of Development Economics, 78*, 443–473.

Weber, A., & Mahringer, H. (2006). *Choice and Success of Job Search Methods.* IZA Discussion Paper No. 1939, Bonn, DE

Wegener, B. (1991). Job Mobility and Social Ties: Social Resources, Prior Job, and Status Attainment. *American Sociological Review, 56*(1), 60–71.

Wielgosz, J. B., & Carpenter, S. (1987). The Effectiveness of Alternative Methods of Searching for Jobs and Finding Them. *American Journal of Economics and Sociology, 46*(2), 151–164.

CHAPTER 7

Pedagogies for Employability of Graduates in the Regional Labour Market

Abstract This chapter discusses trends in pedagogies for employability. It reports on findings of research about the most effective methods for enhancing employability and then explores the relation between the place and pedagogical approaches, considering the value of place awareness for employability potential. Finally, it describes the main features of rural economies and seeks to identify elements there that can support the employability of graduates.

Keywords Self-reflection • Place-based pedagogy • Labour market awareness

7.1 Looking for Models of Intervention

Changes in society and wide-ranging demands and pressures from policies, business, and students have affected teaching and learning. Professors are expected to engage in a spectrum of activities beyond the traditional ones of research and teaching, and to integrate all these tasks into comprehensive pedagogical action. The goal is ambitious, and leaves in the hands of teachers the responsibility for meeting such challenging objectives successfully.

However, there are not many models of intervention to serve as reference schemes for how to design teaching and learning to embed employability throughout the curriculum. One of the best known and probably also the most comprehensive was issued by the Higher Education Academy

G. Paviotti, *'Regional Universities' and Pedagogy*,
https://doi.org/10.1007/978-3-030-53680-0_7

in 2006 (updated in 2012—Pegg et al. 2012), "Pedagogy for employability," which addresses topics such as pedagogical methods, teacher training, and good practices, with reference to the USEM model or tools like the portfolio.

Other contributions have instead focused on the action of teaching, and tried to identify the best ways to provide students with skills and competences for employability purposes.

Pedagogical research regarding employability has mostly focused on the development of soft skills, which has been and still is one of the most debated topics in employability discourse, engaging not only academics but also employers. It is worth recalling that there is no agreed definition of soft, generic, and transversal skills, and there are no reliable assessment methods. However, in general, the literature recognises that the development of generic skills in higher education is favoured by the application of theoretical concepts in real situations where knowledge can be put into practice. To this end, pedagogies based on experiential learning approaches are usually suggested as most suitable. Project-based learning (David 2008) and problem-based learning (Boud and Feletti 1997; Mergendoller et al. 2006) are often indicated as valuable for promoting the acquisition of transversal skills like problem solving (Gallagher et al. 1992), critical thinking (Shepherd 1998), teamwork (Pfaff and Huddleston 2003), and management skills (Kloppenborg and Baucus 2004). In addition, increase in students' generic skills is sought through work-based learning (WBL) or work-integrated learning (WIL), which entail spending a period in a work environment outside university settings and engaging in work-related activities in non-work settings (Frison et al. 2015), for example, volunteering. WBL offers advantages for students, universities, and businesses: it serves pedagogical needs, supports the regional role of universities by increasing links with business through students mobility (Healey 2005; Cyert and Goodman 1997), and provides businesses the opportunity to connect with research and updated methodologies, as well as to evaluate potential future employees in action (Tovey 2001). Finally, students receive the added value of network building with community of practice (as legitimate peripheral participation, Lave and Wenger 1991), and professional contacts useful for job seeking (Brown and Konrad 2001; Tovey 2001).

A crucial point is how learners reflect on and learn from these experiences, which, if exploited well, can enhance meaningful learning, promote the acquisition of generic skills, and build professional networks. Reflective students are in the best position to profit from supplementary learning and work-integrated learning through curricular or non-curricular internships. The active role of students and their capacity for making sense of opportunities are key to the success of any model of intervention, pedagogy or didactic. As Hodgson (1999) pointed out, "Action always takes place in a material and natural integument, but it deals more and more with intersubjective discourses concerning the interpretations, meanings and uses of information" (p. 185). In fact, the literature identifies reflective practices as a "bridge" between the learning offer and actual learning. Rogers (2001) noted shared ideas about the nature of this "bridge" articulated by a variety of authors (Dewey 1933; Schön 1983; Boud et al. 1985; Langer 1989; Loughran 1996; Mezirow 1991; Seibert and Daudelin 1999), who see reflection as a cognitive and affective process that:

> (1) requires active engagement on the part of the individual; (2) is triggered by an unusual or perplexing situation or experience; (3) involves examining one's responses, beliefs, and premises in light of the situation at hand; and (4) results in integration of the new understanding into one's experience. (2001, pp. 41–42)

Reflection underpins the acquisition of high cognitive skills, which is, or should be, the primary mission of the educational journey at tertiary level. It relates to the mediation process between the individual and the world/situation. It shapes the individuality, which, according to Hinchliffe (2006), is "negotiated, constructed and fashioned, and then re-negotiated and re-fashioned again" (p. 98). Reflection requires awareness. In fact, the foundation of any learning experience and identity building is self-awareness, the essential starting point for relating with the world or the Other. Self-awareness is the conscious attention directed to the self, which enables us "to become the object of our own attention and to acknowledge our own existence" (Morin 2002). It allows us to reflect on our own experience following external stimuli (Morin 2011) in different realms of the self (Ben-Artzi et al. 1995). Self-awareness is a state that assumes self-consciousness, both private—related to beliefs, emotions, and so on—and public—related to the self as social object in the context of others' perspective on ourselves or our actions (Fenigstein et al. 1975).

Thus, active pedagogies are useful for supporting career education, and their value will be maximised if they incorporate elements to stimulate self-awareness in students to help them build the "bridge" between the learning experience and its meaning in their life design. Students should be encouraged to consider the importance of place and context as they work to develop their employability.

7.2 Place-based Pedagogy

It is widely acknowledged that situated learning, pedagogical practices in authentic, real-world settings, promotes active learning. Context-based pedagogies support transformative learning (Mezirow 1991) and self-awareness processes. They allow students to navigate across domains of knowledge and discourse and re-formulate meanings through a mediation process between themselves and the world. In this Third Space of learning, employability and pre-professionalism can also be constructed (Fink 2003; Moje et al. 2004; Jill 2008). The concept of Third Space has been formulated in geographical research by Lefevre (1974) as "space of representation [...] [that] can also be perceived as 'lived space' ", the one in which we give meaning, that includes the "first space" (perceived) and the "second space" (cognitively constructed) (Soja 1996). Employability and pre-professionalism can also be constructed in this Third Space of learning (Fink 2003; Moje et al. 2004; Jill 2008), a "space of representation [...] [that] can also be perceived as 'lived space' ", the one in which we give meaning, that includes the "first space" (perceived) and the "second space" (cognitively constructed) (Soja 1996). In the educational field, the work of Gutiérrez et al. 1999a, 2008, 2014) stresses the significance of "hybrid spaces" of learning, as "mediational context and tools necessary for future social and cognitive development" (Gutiérrez et al. 1999a, p. 92). In this hybrid space, different codes meet and dialogue, stimulating "processes of elaboration of meaning among those who share codes and strive to achieve a common understanding" (p. 88). Scholars attribute to space and place very different meaning and nuances that will be not explored fully here. In Gutiérrez's sense, the place is the social context where "people make places and places make people" (Gruenewald 2003a). Therefore, designing learning in context means putting students to work in a place, that is, providing hybrid spaces for learning in places "for participation with the phenomenal, ecological, and cultural world" (Gruenewald, p. 646).

Place-based education, also defined in philosophical terms as place-conscious education, has been mostly debated in the school system, and in the US context. Proponents seek the integration of education and the cultural and ecological integrity of lived places (Somerville 2007) by considering that learning takes place also outside school, within the community (Holt 1989). In this context, Smith (2002) proposed five approaches to place-based learning to embed educational research with place practices, namely: (a) local cultural studies, (b) local nature studies, (c) community issue-investigation and problem-solving, (d) local internships and entrepreneurial opportunities, and (e) induction into community decision making. In one form or another, all can have an added value for employability, according to taught disciplines, also in higher education. Gruenewald (2003b) discussed relations between critical pedagogy and place-based pedagogies, asserting that a "critical pedagogy of places" would offer the opportunity for "challenging each other to read the texts of our own lives and to ask constantly what needs to be transformed and what needs to be conserved" (p. 10). Opportunities arising from Gruenewald's developmental idea are also significant in higher education: such an approach would combine regional research and experiential, place-based learning. In addition, it would add value to place-based employability by strengthening the links with the territory.

In fact, place-based learning design often takes the form of co-design with a "territory", referring to the definition of Torre and Wallet (2016):

> Territories are collective productions of a human community, with citizens, governance structures and organizations, and are not merely geographic entities; they are formed of a combination of individuals and/or stakeholders located within areas whose boundaries may shift according to their interactions. (p. 23)

Co-design with the territory means in this sense co-creation with a large and diverse group of stakeholders, including public and private companies, associations, NGOs, and others.

Co-design of learning involves a deeper relationship with the stakeholder, who is not merely the host, but an active part of the process. For example, a project-based learning process with companies requires time, effort, and learning design from both sides; even if the teacher defines learning outcomes and techniques, the firm contributes with content (and time). Through experiential activities, students get in touch with the real world. Not only do they learn the subject and engage in meaning-making, but they also gain increased awareness of the context, that is, the environment, cultural values, and employment culture of the place. They learn the features of the place and, through self-reflection, evaluate their capitals and develop well-reasoned employability plans.

7.3 Pursuing Employability for Rural Labour Markets

The employability narrative is based on the idea that one size fits all. Instead, research has provided evidence of the role played by other factors in employability potential, such as a disadvantaged background. In addition, it appears clear that diversity, specialisation, and culture shape the work environment just as they shape territories and regions. A graduate's prospects for employment are also influenced by where her home is, and where she might prefer to live. Pedagogy is not an independent variable either: learning design is made according to subjects, learners, needs, and places. Employability is not a separate study subject: it refers to a process of life design in which the subject considers internal and external factors and seeks to balance personal ambitions and wishes with external opportunities and possibilities. Skills and preparation for work play a crucial role: these are the starting point for building any professional project. However, other capitals as defined by Tomlinson (2017) play an equal role. Being skilled is not enough.

This book focuses on the issue of graduate employability in the challenging contexts of regional and mostly rural labour markets, which for the most part are marked by low technology–based economies with underdeveloped service sectors that provide predominantly low-skill occupations. We have seen how recruitment methods differ according to the size of the company: in rural economies, businesses tend to use informal recruiting channels. Also, the entrepreneurial culture of a place affects entrepreneurial intentions (Huggins and Thompson 2015), and the lack of infrastructure in rural areas also hinders the establishment of new companies.

In addition, the "rural culture" and other place-based, cultural factors affect recruitment and retention. Table 7.1 presents the key features of local labour markets in rural economies and how graduates can face these challenges:

Obviously, a student's employability potential is not determined exclusively by academic preparation: it is also affected by the student's personal and social needs. Those who would feel more fulfilled by remaining in

Table 7.1 Rural labour markets and actions that graduates may take

Features or local labour markets	*Actions that graduates may take*
Underdeveloped service sector	Transfer of competences in another sector
Work experience required (no time for company training)	Gain experience as possible during the study years (through internship or seasonal, intermittent work)
Strong (family) and weak (friends, neighbours) ties are crucial for recruiting	Building networks during the university years
Preponderance of SMEs	Building networks and establish relations during the study years
Preponderance of family business	Consider entrepreneurship; prepare a plan during the university years

their rural areas close to family and friends must take into account the extra difficulties of finding employment in these settings. They may be so absorbed in "the global" experience of university, the media, and internet that they fail to be realistic in building employability strategies that consider the economic reality of rural settings and in envisioning how their personal choice to "stay rural" may impact their professional outcomes. In this context, universities should support their students in becoming more employable by providing them as many opportunities as possible to develop hard and soft skills, and to make informed, aware, and well-reasoned decisions.

Placed-based pedagogy can support this process by supplementing the normal educational objectives, skills acquisition, and curricula with input to help students gain awareness about complicated and difficult labour markets, especially in the case of universities that serve disadvantaged, remote, and rural areas. They can provide ways for students to gain insight into the business culture of the place and learn about its work ethos. This provides students with a competitive advantage and enables them to plan ahead to avoid being "lost in transition" as they transition from academia to the world of work.

In this context, also education to foster entrepreneurship is an important aspect of employability development. Such input may not necessarily lead graduates to launch their own businesses, but it would at least broaden their horizons to consider another avenue for possible employment.

Does pedagogy explicitly designed for rural areas exist? If not, should it? Probably not as such. However, place counts very much in employment outcomes, and pedagogy in "regional university" should be the subject of a higher level of debate and research.

References

Ben-Artzi, E., Mikulincer, M., & Glaubman, H. (1995). The Multifaceted Nature of Self-Consciousness: Conceptualization, Measurement, and Consequences. *Imagination, Cognition and Personality, 15*(1), 17–43.

Boud, D., & Feletti, G. (1997). *The Challenge of Problem-based Learning* (2nd ed.). London: Kogan.

Boud, D., Keogh, R., & Walker, D. (1985). Promoting Reflection in Learning: A Model. In D. Boud, R. Keogh, & D. Walker (Eds.), *Reflection: Turning Experience Into Learning* (pp. 18–40). London: Kogan Page.

Brown, D. W., & Konrad, A. M. (2001). Granovetter Was Right: The Importance of Weak Ties to a Contemporary Job Search. *Group & Organization Management, 26*(4), 434–462.

Cyert, R. M., & Goodman, P. S. (1997). Creating Effective University-Industry Alliances: An Organizational Learning Perspective. *Organizational Dynamics, 25*(4), 45–57.

David, J. L. (2008). What Research Says About/Project-Based Learning. *Educational Leadership Teaching Students to Think, 65*(5), 80–82.

Dewey, J. (1933). *How We Think: A Restatement of the Relation of Reflective Thinking to the Educative Process.* Boston: D.C. Heath.

Fenigstein, A., Scheier, M. F., & Buss, A. H. (1975). Public and Private Self-consciousness: Assessment and Theory. *Journal of Consulting and Clinical Psychology, 43*, 522–527.

Fink, L. (2003). *Creating Significant Learning Experiences.* San Francisco, CA: Jossey-Bass.

Frison, D., Fedeli, M., & Taylor, E. W. (2015). Work-Related Learning: A Survey on Teaching and Learning Methods in the Italian Higher Education System. *ICERI 2015 Proceedings*, pp. 8393–8401.

Gallagher, S. A., Stepien, W. J., & Rosenthal, H. (1992). The Effects of Problem-Based Learning on Problem Solving. *Gifted Child Quarterly, 36*(4), 195–200.

Gruenewald, D. A. (2003a). Foundations of Place: A Multidisciplinary Framework for Place-Conscious Education. *American Educational Research Journal, 40*(3), 619–654.

Gruenewald, D. A. (2003b). The Best of Both Worlds: A Critical Pedagogy of Place. *Educational Researcher, 32*(4), 3–12.

Gutiérrez, K. D. (2008). Developing a Sociocritical Literacy in the Third Space. *Reading Research Quarterly, 43*(2), 148–164.

Gutiérrez, K. D., Baquedano-López, P., Alvarez, H., & Chiu, M. M. (1999a). Building a Culture of Collaboration Through Hybrid Language Practices. *Theory Into Practice, 38*, 87–93.

Gutiérrez, K. D., Baquedano-López, P., & Tejeda, C. (1999b). Rethinking Diversity: Hybridity and Hybrid Language Practices in the Third Space. *Mind, Culture, and Activity, 6*(4), 286–303.

Gutiérrez, K. D., Penuel, W. R., & W.R. (2014). Relevance to Practice as a Criterion for Rigor. *Educational Researcher, 43*(1), 19–23.

Healey, M. (2005). Linking Research and Teaching to Benefit Student Learning. *Journal of Geography in Higher Education, 29*(2), 183–201.

Hinchliffe, G. (2006). Graduate Employability and Lifelong Learning: A Need for Realism? In P. Hager & S. Holland (Eds.), *Graduate Attributes, Learning and Employability*. Dordrecht: Springer.

Hodgson, G. (1999). *Economics and Utopia. Why the Learning Economy Is Not the End of History*. London: Routledge.

Holt, J. (1989). *Learning All the Time*. Reading, MA: Addison-Wesley.

Huggins, R., & Thompson, P. (2015). Culture and Place-Based Development: A Socio-Economic Analysis. *Regional Studies, 49*(1), 130–159.

Jill, F. M. (2008). A Pedagogical Model of Higher Education/Industry Engagement for Enhancing Employability and Professional Practice. *Proceedings Work Integrated Learning (WIL): Transforming Futures, Practice... Pedagogy...Partnerships*, pp. 164–169, Manly, Sydney, Australia

Kloppenborg, T. J., & Baucus, M. S. (2004). Project Management in Local Non-profit Organizations: Engaging Students in Problem based Learning. *Journal of Management Education, 28*, 610–630.

Langer, E. J. (1989). *Mindfulness*. Reading, MA: Addison-Wesley Publishing.

Lave, J., & Wenger, E. (1991). *Situated Learning. Legitimate Peripheral Participation*. Cambridge: Cambridge University Press.

Lefevre, H. (1974). *The Production of Space* (D. Nicholson-Smith from "Production de l'espace", 1974, Trans.). Cambridge, MA: Basil Blackwell Ltd., 1991.

Loughran, J. J. (1996). *Developing Reflective Practice: Learning about Teaching and Learning Through Modeling*. Washington, DC: Falmer Press.

Mergendoller, J. R., Markham, T., Ravitz, J., & Larmer, J. (2006). Pervasive Management of Project Based Learning. Teachers as Guides and Facilitator. In C. M. Evertson & C. S. Weinstein (Eds.), *Handbook of Classroom Management: Research, Practice, and Contemporary Issues*. London: Routledge.

Mezirow, J. (1991). *Transformative Dimensions of Adult Learning*. San Francisco: Jossey-Bass.

Moje, E. B., McIntosh Chiechanowski, K., Kramer, K. E., Ellis, L., Carrillo, R., & Collazo, T. (2004). Working Toward Third Space in Content Area Literacy: An Examination of Everyday Funds of Knowledge and Discourse. *Reading Research Quarterly, 39*(1), 38–70.

Morin, A. (2002). Self-Awareness Review Part 1: Do You "Self-Reflect" or "Self-Ruminate"? *Science & Consciousness Review*, December, No. 1.

Morin, A. (2011). Self-Awareness Part 1: Definition, Measures, Effects, Functions, and Antecedents. *Social and Personality Psychology Compass, 5*(10), 807.

Pegg, A., Waldock, J., Hendy-Isaac, S., & Lawton, R. (2012). *Pedagogies for Employability*. York: The Higher Education Academy.

Pfaff, E., & Huddleston, P. (2003). Does It Matter if I Hate Teamwork? What Impacts Student Attitudes Toward Teamwork. *Journal of Marketing Education, 25*, 37–45.

Schön, D. A. (1983). *The Reflective Practitioner: How Professionals Think in Action*. New York: Basic Books.

Seibert, K. W., & Daudelin, M. W. (1999). *The Role of Reflection in Managerial Learning: Theory, Research, and Practice*. Westport, CT: Quorum.

Shepherd, H. G. (1998). The Probe Method: A Problem-based Learning Model's Effect on Critical Thinking Skills of Fourth and Fifth Grade Social Studies Students. Dissertation Abstracts International Section A Humanities and Social Sciences, 59(3–A), 0799.

Smith, G. (2002). Place-based Education: Learning to be Where We Are. *Phi Delta Kappan, 83*, 584–594.

Soja, E. W. (1996). *Thirdspace. Journeys to Los Angeles and Other Real-Imagined Places*. Cambridge, MA: Blackwell Publishers.

Somerville, M. J. (2007). A Place Pedagogy for 'Global Contemporaneity'. *Educational Philosophy and Theory, 42*(3), 326.

Tomlinson, M. (2017). Forms of Graduate Capital and Their Relationship to Graduate Employability. *Education + Training, 59*(4), 338–352.

Torre, A., & Wallet, F. (2016). *Regional Development in Rural Areas* (SpringerBriefs in Regional Science). Springer.

Tovey, J. (2001). Building Connections between Industry and University: Implementing an Internship Program at a Regional University. *Technical Communication Quarterly, 10*(2), 225–239.

Conclusions

This book provides an initial exploration of a complex topic that requires greater attention. The low levels of employment of university graduates in rural regions seem to have been accepted as a given, not as an issue to be remedied through policies and practices. Discourse about employability addresses the topic in the overall framework of "geographical disadvantage", and policymakers focus on rural development, the regional roles of universities, or the employability of graduates. Instead, the links between these different aspects remain to be clarified. Sustainability is the overarching goal of human society, as we all need to work towards an environmentally, economically, and socially sustainable future for the world: it is assumed that decent work for all and sustainable communities also includes sustainability of rural communities.

Stereotypes still tend to define "the rural" as full of potential for development and job creation on the one hand, while simultaneously disadvantaged and deprived on the other. While the European Union has established development policies and appropriated funding to execute them, rural and peripheral areas still suffer from the phenomenon of depopulation. In particular, young people leave the countryside in search of better work prospects, or even for job opportunities for which they are over-graduated and over-skilled, as they are unable find any position at all.

How can rural communities be sustainable if deprived of the younger and most educated segment of the population? How can cities be smart and environmentally responsible if they steadily grow as the main and

G. Paviotti, *'Regional Universities' and Pedagogy*,
https://doi.org/10.1007/978-3-030-53680-0

sometimes only centres of work and services? Finally, how can we work towards major goals of sustainability without the adoption of system-level thinking, based on actual and constructive dialogue both at the vertical level of policies and at the horizontal one of stakes in society?

The literature has already debated many issues, and we have many research results from which it is possible to start re-framing the picture of employment and employability. Current narratives do not apply equally across Europe, or even at the levels of member states. Place-based approaches are promising, but have yet to be exploited in policies and practices. Sometimes policies do not support practices, as in the case of the education system, often asked to be committed locally, while being evaluated nationally according to different indicators. The topic of the employability of graduates is marked by several contrasts. On the one hand, universities are asked to educate "employable graduates" but are not in the position to provide on-the-job training, a vital part of the development of professionalism. On the other hand, companies are under pressure to survive in a global market, and their requests are increasingly sophisticated in terms of skills, flexibility, and adaptability. Small or medium enterprises in particular claim they lack the time and resources for training new staff. They are often hampered by a limited understanding of which skills they actually need in their workplaces, and fail to grasp the reasons they cannot find suitable staff. Also, in general, there are no shared definitions for concepts like employability skills, transversal skills, and work-readiness, and this makes dialogue among different actors even more problematic. Finally, the meaning of sustainability and innovation is also amorphous, with definitions that vary according to the context.

Policies seem to focus on major sustainability goals which for the most part are evident needs of the global world: however, often there is a misalignment between objectives, programming, and implementation, so the outcome is less encouraging than expected.

Universities in undeveloped regions or areas characterised by rural labour markets are expected to achieve the same outcomes as those in cities and developed regions. However, a university's contribution to local innovation through its research, or its effectiveness in preparing employable graduates, must necessarily derive from a particular approach, and achieve different outcomes, according to its location. But for both rural and urban universities, it is not enough to provide skills and inform students about "business culture" as a general understanding of how the market works, and then leave the responsibility of "being employable" to the students alone. Also, universities should not be expected to replace guidance centres, employment services, or training institutions in functions supporting access to work. Acknowledging that roles and functions change as society evolves, there should be shared responsibility for the components of employability, just as there is for sustainable development goals.

The dual labour market is socially and economically unsustainable, as is the constant exodus from rural to urban areas, and the flow of workers from southern to northern parts of countries and from southern nations to northern ones in Europe. The current pandemic has also made it painfully evident that the European social model is at risk. According to current figures, many European countries will suffer severe economic crisis: the effects of the downturn will not be shared equally across the workforce, and there will be differences between protected and precarious workers, and between the employed and those trying to find work. It is likely that young people will again be the weaker segment of the workforce and of society.

No one single recipe exists for addressing such a complex issue: no one-size-fits-all model can answer questions coming from the cultural, economic, and social richness and diversity of Europe. However, some questions, including the development of rural areas in terms of high-skilled job, job retention, and the creation of sustainable rural communities, should find their place as a topic under discussion. Accordingly, more dialogue is needed among researchers from different fields to identify possible sustainable development pathways. We need to build spaces of understanding and debate in order to contribute to society through research.

Universities struggle under the weight of many burdens, and the higher-education system has received numerous requests from many sides. Those who work in the university environment are aware of its limits, conflicts, and contradictions. However, there are also further opportunities to support our students in their life journey. While the university cannot meet requests to "solve problems" in areas for which it has little capacity for action, such as the features of the labour market, there are still spaces of intervention for individual students through well-designed pedagogy.

In this context, the overall goal of education should also be questioned. Is it simply a matter of "producing employable individuals"? We would argue that a greater aspiration should guide our efforts, that of educating "aware citizens" who promote in society the higher values of democracy, equality, and social justice. In the present cultural and social environment, work is one of the citizens' main expressions and contributions to society, and graduates, as its most educated members, should be enabled to express their higher skills in any context and situation, while they also promote these higher values. For this, the context, the place, is of paramount importance: understanding and interpreting reality also apply to the work environment, which has a strong cultural component and specific dynamics. We cannot assume that positive inputs from the university will always ensure graduates' success in finding and retaining work where they desire to live. They may have to leave the countryside, or their country, not because they want to go, but because they cannot find a way to build a life there. It is to be hoped that university efforts to build increased awareness of the place into its pedagogy to enhance employability will help students think more strategically as they manage their transition from academia to the world of work, and, in the final analysis, increase their capacity to deal with and work to improve the world as they find it, not to passively resent it for not being what they imagined it should be.

This book has reached its final version during the COVID-19 pandemic. As European and world societies, we are facing difficult times that may well worsen before they improve. There is a risk that we may simply yearn to restore the pre-pandemic status quo. Instead, higher education is making its contribution not only to the challenge of overcoming the economic crisis, but also to finding for the future more environmentally, economically, and socially sustainable ways of living and working that support the higher goals of democracy, equality, and social justice.

Index

G. Paviotti, *'Regional Universities' and Pedagogy*,
https://doi.org/10.1007/978-3-030-53680-0

The manufacturer's authorised representative in the EU is Springer Nature Customer Service Centre GmbH, Europaplatz 3, 69115 Heidelberg, Germany. If you have any concerns regarding our products, please contact ProductSafety@springernature.com

Printed and bound by CPI Group (UK) Ltd, Croydon, CR0 4YY
30/09/2026
02225339-0001